Recession, The Western Economies and the Changing World Order

Recession, The Western Economies and the Changing World Order

Lars Anell

HF
1411
.A494
1981B

Frances Pinter Ltd
London

First Published in Great Britain in 1981 by
Frances Pinter (Publishers) Ltd
5 Dryden Street, London WC2E 9NW

ISBN 0 903804 94 8

Translated by John and Peter Hogg (Chs I-IV & VI)
and Mona Morris Nygren (Chapter V)

Typeset by Donald Typesetting, Bristol
Printed in Great Britain by A. Wheaton & Co., Exeter

CONTENTS

The definition of "billion" used throughout is one thousand million.

PREFACE

What actually is an international economic order? How does it function? Which are its cohesive forces? What are the pre-requisites for establishing a stable economic world order during the remainder of this century? These are some of the questions that are of central significance in this book.

In an earlier study I indicated that 'the growing international disorder now evident is not principally a question of interstate relations. The unwillingness or incapacity of the states to adhere to the established rules has national causes' (1). The former stability which characterized the 1960s coincided with a rapid and steady economic growth. This enabled governments to deal with the demands of different interest groups within a fairly generous framework. The question, however, is whether it is a stable order which permits rapid growth, or the annual increase in the government's 'elbow-room' which makes a certain order possible.

It is these reflections that are pursued in the present study. Chap. II describes the unique pre-conditions for the international order during the long period from the end of the war until the early 1970s. In a number of respects evident changes have now taken place. Factors contributing to this include both the acute economic crisis during the 1970s (chap. III) and the long-term structural changes in the international economic system (chap. IV). For that reason it becomes more difficult to maintain the rules of the game for the international economy, both politically and from a technical-administrative viewpoint.

The relationship between the nation state and the international order is dealt with in chap. V. Attention is focused on the role of the government in the so-called welfare states. A pre-requisite for the participation of a country in a world order is that the national economy is adapted in accordance with the existing rules of play. This presupposes that the government can persuade, entice, or force its citizens to accept the discipline that is required. The question discussed in chap. V is above all

1. Anell & Nygren, p. 155.

whether the governments in the OECD countries have this power to take long-term rational decisions.

Chap. I deals chiefly with questions of definitions and theoretical perspectives. Among other things I point to the implications of the fact that an order is a public good. The final chapter deals with the prerequisites for re-establishing a stable free-trade order during the twentieth century, and the alternatives that may be available.

I wish to convey my warm thanks for valuable comments to Carl Hamilton, Lars Ingelstam, Lennart Klackenberg, Mans Lonnroth, and Staffan Sohlman, and for help with typing the draft to Margareta Granas, Lena Kjellstrom, and Lis-Beth Olsson. Per Lennart Borjesson contributed in a most valuable way in working out part of the statistical material for chap. V. My wife has greatly improved the editing of the book. Finally, I am also indebted to Mona Morris Nygren for numerous refinements of the stylistic presentation. The responsibility for errors or shortcomings which might remain is of course entirely my own.

Finally, I wish to thank the Swedish Secretariat for Future Studies and the International Centre of the Swedish Labour Movement for having generously contributed to financing the translation of this study (2).

Lars Anell
Stockholm, September 1980

2. This study is part of the project 'Sweden in a new international economic order', sponsored by the Swedish Secretariat for Future Studies. Originally it was published in Swedish in January 1980. For the English edition the final chapter has been considerably revised and enlarged.

Our conclusion ... is that this society and the industrialized world in general, is simultaneously undergoing a conceptual revolution as thorough-going in its effects as the Copernican Revolution, and an institutional revolution as profound as the Industrial Revolution. Furthermore, this overall transformation is proceeding with extreme rapidity, such that the most critical period will be passed through within a decade. Whether the social structure can withstand the strain is very much at issue, and that will greatly depend on how well we can understand the nature and necessity of the transformation as we experience it.

Willis W. Harman

I. ON THE CONCEPT OF AN ECONOMIC WORLD ORDER – SOME THEORETICAL POINTS OF DEPARTURE

> Confusion is a word we have invented for an order which is not understood.
>
> *Henry Miller*

> Watch out for the fellow who talks about putting things in order. Putting things in order always means getting other people under your control.
>
> *Denis Diderot*

The economic co-operation between the states of the world is based on certain rules which together constitute an international economic order. In this book attention will be directed primarily to a discussion of the forces that sustain and hold together such a system of rules. To start with, however, we must try to provide a definition of the concept of an economic order.

Definition

In an earlier context I have defined the concept of an international economic order as 'the rules that regulate the economic co-operation of sovereign states in different spheres and are maintained by the existing distribution of power' (1). The aim

1. Anell & Nygren, p. 141.

of that definition was partly to establish the principal function of an order, partly to indicate that an order must be based on the existing power structure.

That definition is not appropriate in the present context. We shall be discussing below the possibility of maintaining an order in a world economy that lacks a dominant power centre. Furthermore, an order does not have to reflect exactly the distribution of power. Individual countries possess different forms of power and means of power. They may also assess the need for an order in different ways.

We shall therefore adopt a simpler and less restrictive definition. A world economic order will in the present context refer to *the rules and norms applying to international economic cooperation*.

The expression 'rules and norms' makes it clear that an order can be governed both by written and unwritten components. The circumstance that the world order during the postwar period has to an uncommon extent been governed by written rules is to be explained mainly by the fact that it was elaborated as a blueprint within the American administration *before* it was applied in practice. In addition, the government of the United States needed to account for its plans to Congress and had a general weakness for written rules. In contrast to this, the *pax Britannica* during the century before the First World War was almost wholly based on codified practice.

Now, the important thing is not whether a rule is written or unwritten but that it is valid in the sense that it is actually applied and obeyed. As a matter of fact, however, no rule — whether international or national — is obeyed completely. What is meant here is that an order is 'applied' when its rules are obeyed to such an extent that the participants base their actions on the supposition that other agents respect the rules of the game.

Validity is thus a matter of grading. What is significant, however, is that the degree of application must be very high. Presumably one must expect breaches of the rules to amount only to a few per cent in order to be able to talk of a well-functioning order. This can be exemplified by the 'street order' in certain major cities. Robberies are still rare even in insecure areas of New York. And yet the likelihood is assessed as sufficiently great for people to alter their behaviour. They avoid walking about after dark. The order has ceased to operate despite the fact that the risk of being robbed is small.

In this particular case, however, the cost of altering one's behaviour — i.e. giving up the evening stroll — is fairly low while, at the same time, to run the risk that the order is not applied involves mortal danger.

To business enterprises in a competitive situation the matter looks somewhat different. The cost of totally abstaining from new investments is very high. In expanding branches with rapid technological development, new investments are necessary for an enterprise to survive. Nor is insecurity a radically new experience for business enterprises; a more unstable order simply means that the insecurity increases.

We must therefore expect firms to modify their behaviour only if the order becomes more unstable. This may in itself constitute a great economic loss to the world community, however, since it will very probably mean that given resources are exploited less efficiently than would be possible in a more stable order.

Now, which are the spheres of activity covered by our definition of an international economic order? When the world economic order of the postwar period was elaborated, attention was concentrated on trade, investments, international capital movements, credit, and foreign exchange questions. It is obvious that shipping questions also belong in the international sphere, as do international agreements, for example on outer space, copyright, and patents. Yet at the core of international co-operation are still the rules and norms governing the location of investments and the organization of international trade.

The problem is that questions previously regarded as national have acquired an increasingly evident international dimension. This relates above all to stabilization policies and demand management. At the latest summit meetings of the world's seven leading industrial nations the co-ordination of their economic policies has been at the forefront. Several economists look upon such co-ordination as a precondition for a functioning international order. 'Both the logic of analysis and the evidence from recent experiences indicate that, despite the partial buffer provided by managed flexibility of exchange rates, tension persists between the vulnerability created by increasing market integration and the fragmentation of policy formation. If we do not find ways to co-ordinate policies, we will inevitably slip backward from market integration' (2).

The interdependence between national economies, the tension between increased integration and demands for the preservation of national autonomy, are the decisive problems in attempts to maintain an international order. These questions will be dealt with in detail in chap. V. For the time being we shall leave the definition as it stands, although the limits of what constitutes international co-operation have not been clearly demarcated. It should finally be added that the discussion that follows applies chiefly to the international order for the world's *market economies*.

Order and stability

An international economic order consists of a number of more or less well-functioning sub-orders. Some of these are mutually dependent. This is the case, for instance, in regard to trade and international payments. No genuine free trade can be conceived of without a monetary system in which currencies from different countries are convertible. Other aspects of the order are more independent.

One should also distinguish between superordinate principles governing several or all areas, and more specific rules. Examples of general basic rules are that states respect each other's sovereignty and that agreements are to be honoured, as well as the rules on private ownership. We shall later touch on the question whether these principles will also have universal validity in the future. So far, however, these rules have been valid in all spheres, while the most favoured-nation principle, for instance, is a specific trade rule.

The main function of an order is to make the future behaviour of states and business enterprises predictable. This does not

2. Whitman, p. 27.

necessarily mean that rules and behaviour must remain un-changed. It is important, on the other hand, to be able to foresee the direction that changes will take and their expected scope. The order of the postwar period has changed radically in several respects during a relatively short time. And yet the order apply-ing up to the beginning of the 1970s was very stable. The reason for this is that the changes that occurred took a specific and predictable direction. As early as the 1940s it was evident that world trade would become increasingly free. Stability in this situation therefore meant that developments could on the whole be predicted. Investing enterprises could rely in their calculations on gradually improving trading conditions.

I would finally like to insist that the concept of order should be seen as neutral in regard to values. It is true that an order has intrinsic value in the sense that it allows a more effective inter-national division of labour, according to traditional economic theory. One should, nevertheless, generally view systems of rules as means to achieve particular goals.

A certain order can function extremely well without there being unanimity on the results that are achieved. During the postwar period we have had an order which functioned well, at least 'technically', for fifteen to twenty years. The majority of governments in the world have, however, clearly asserted that they regard this order to be biased in favour of the established industrial countries. Many would certainly also maintain that it is cynical to speak of a functioning world order while, at the same time, hundreds of millions of people live in direst need, starvation, and poverty. That an order may be unjust is one thing, however. That it functions in a technical sense is another. It is quite possible to talk of a mechanism functioning, without approving of the result it produces.

Quite another matter is that it may be difficult in the future to reach unanimity about this mechanism if the different coun-tries in the world have clearly divergent opinions about the kind of development that should be promoted.

Order as a public good

Even Adam Smith, in his time, evolved a theory for what political economists call public goods or utilities. A characteristic of these is that they cannot be reserved exclusively for the consumption of a particular individual or group. If a country strengthens its defence, this involves protection for all its citizens. The same applies to a public road. When the road has been completed, everyone can make use of it. Law and order also constitute a typical public good; measures taken by society to eliminate the risk of attacks in the street produce advantages for all lawabiding citizens. The problem with public goods is that they can be utilized whether one pays or not. Once the commodity has been produced, it can be used by everyone — and those who can will naturally avoid paying. This is assumed to lead to a lower output of public goods than would be desirable for society as a whole.

On the national level the problem has usually been solved in such a way that all citizens pay taxes to 'produce' public goods like defence, roads, culture, and law and order. The government takes on the responsibility for deciding how much is needed and how it is to be paid for. In addition there is a national system of sanctions to regulate the right to make use of public goods. Within nations the opportunities for using a collective commodity without paying, 'taking a free ride', are strictly limited.

On the international level there is no accepted system for obtaining repayment and prosecuting for infringements. The question is how one will be able in the future to 'produce' the utility known as international economic order on an adequate scale. So far during the postwar period this has been done in a particular way that offers hardly any guarantees for the future.

The economic order of the postwar period was formulated within the American administration. The dominant role of the United States in the economy of the Western world was self-evident at the end of the war and was accepted by the other OECD countries. The overriding concern of Washington related to security policy. The United States took it upon itself to guarantee the security of the so-called free world, whether this was wanted or not. Reconstruction in Europe and Japan became a strategic part of the battle against Communism. In the economic sphere the Americans were therefore prepared to accept a fair amount of 'free-riding'. The Japanese, for instance, were allowed to carry out their export offensive without having to 'pay their way' by facilitating imports.

To some degree, however, this order was financed by the ability of the United States to 'tax' the rest of the world. The American dollar was the dominant currency. The United States assumed the role of central bank for the world, and derived considerable economic advantages from this. The rest of the world was supplied annually with dollars corresponding to the deficits in the American balance of payments. With these dollars the United States paid for part of its imports from abroad. At a cost corresponding to the expense of printing dollar bills the Americans could acquire real resources from the rest of the world. During the 1950s the profit was small but, as the costs of the Vietnam War rose, the deficits in the balance of payments grew rapidly. By the beginning of the 1970s the rest of the world had accumulated enormous dollar holdings, which represented a short-term claim on the American economy. But then the foreign exchange rates were allowed to float, with the result that the United States' debt was written off concurrently with the fall in the exchange rate of the dollar (3).

As we have noted, Japan and the European OECD countries accepted the leading role of the United States. More important, however, the American order promoted the desired development — rapid growth and full employment.

This order was thus based on preconditions unique in several respects. One state was accepted as leader by the others and was able to impose a levy on them. The leading states had partly *differing* goals and this *facilitated* the maintenance of the order. The United States held an economic position that permitted, and a political interest that conceded, a certain free-riding by other countries.

As late as the 1960s the world order was a matter of concern only for a few countries that shared largely the same cultural and economic values. This was quite essential, as a public good is always part of a social structure. Within a single country it is the existing power relations that decide who is to pay and who derives most benefit from collective goals such as defence, roads, the judicial system, and law and order. The dominant position

---

3. During the years 1970–4 West Germany's dollar holdings depreciated by one-third when the value of the dollar decreased by 53 per cent against the D-mark (Hudson, p. 30).

of a small group of industrial countries and their strong common interest in free trade have thus contributed to the stability of the postwar period.

None of these unique preconditions will apply in the future. Let us therefore look at some general prerequisites for maintaining an international order.

A primary basic condition is that the participants have a stake in the maintenance of a given order. The system must provide some *advantage* that outweighs the costs normally associated with participation.

The relationship between advantages and disadvantages is complicated by the fact that the advantages are often general and diffuse while the costs may be very tangible.

International free trade permits effective utilization of given resources of production. Production in all participating countries increases more rapidly than would otherwise be possible. But it is difficult to trace the advantages to particular groups. The gains from free trade are anonymous and are often taken for granted.

Costs, on the other hand, may be very tangible. A factory has to be closed down; the reason is said to be that imports from so-called low-wage countries make it impossible to keep it running. Only rarely, as we know, is the blame laid on an incompetent director or a lazy marketing manager. Low-wage imports are made the scapegoat for far more than they deserve. Import controls or subsidies would in this case produce obvious advantages for one group of people, one locality, and one region, while the loss of welfare due to such measures is small and diluted.

In addition, the effects of free trade are usually unfair. It is primarily the weak regions and the worst-off groups that are affected. The theory is obviously that the gains from free trade will suffice to compensate those who are affected. This does not always happen, however. The new jobs may not suit the people who have lost their old ones. Nor is the loss of a job and social environment always compensated for by a new job and higher wage.

For these reasons the gains must probably be considerably higher than the costs if the citizens of a given country are willingly to accept free trade as an effective and legitimate system.

A second central condition is that participating countries act with awareness of how vulnerable the international order is. When free-riding reaches a certain level, production of the universally desired public good ceases.

The relationship of a country to the order is determined by its role in the world economy. Only one or a few countries — in the present circumstances the United States or the European Economic Community (EEC) — can be said to have what is called structural power, i.e. the ability to positively alter the rules (4). But many countries are able to wreck the system, and a sufficient number of small countries can collectively disrupt the order. An example of this was the action taken by Belgium, the Netherlands, and Switzerland in converting their sterling holdings in the summer of 1931. The collapse of the monetary system was thereby accelerated (5).

One complication is that the dependence of countries on a certain order varies. The American market is sufficiently large for autarchy to be a feasible *economic* alternative to continued free trade. The EEC countries collectively are also able to offer a market that provides acceptable advantages of large-scale production and competition. The dependence of individual EEC countries on the developing countries as a market has, however, increased greatly during the 1970s. The West German economy in particular is heavily dependent on exports. Japan's need for oil, aluminium, wheat, and soya beans is met 90-100 per cent by imports. About a quarter of all foodstuffs are bought by Japan from abroad, and the large corporations are heavily dependent on exports. For smaller industrial countries like Sweden, Austria, and Switzerland the external dependence is similar to that of Japan.

These varying relationships of dependence should naturally govern the liability to pay for the collective utility. This is hardly the case, however. Japan is the country that has been permitted most free-riding because the United States has had a strategic interest in promoting a strong Japanese economy. The

4. Cohen, quoted in *Interfutures*, differentiates between structural power (the ability to determine rules) and procedural power (the ability to make use of given rules).
5. Calleo, pp. 21-3.

cold war has contributed to 'financing' the economic order. It will probably be necessary for both the United States and the EEC to have strategic secondary interests for the future in order to make it possible to organize the 'payment liability' for a functioning free-trade order.

Cohesive forces

In a concluding section we shall discuss the prerequisites for preserving or maintaining an international economic order. Here only a brief indication will be given of some of the methods available for sustaining an order. The methods that are conceivable may be seen in five different dimensions which in no way exclude each other:

a) altruistic orders
b) orders based on enlightened self-interest
c) orders based on clear systems of rules
d) hegemonic orders
e) regional orders

It would appear over-optimistic to suggest altruism as a method of maintaining an order. It is too obvious that a world order cannot be based on this method. It should be remembered, however, that altruistic behaviour does occur. Certain small countries provide international aid on a scale that can hardly be explained by 'rational cost calculations'. The willingness to support the UN in various contexts also has altruistic elements. Elements of altruism are important because they facilitate efforts to maintain an order.

Within a small group, free-riding is strictly limited by social control. In larger and more fragmented groups the social control decreases and the demands for systems of sanctions increase. The difficulties with a global system that is *exclusively* based on enlightened self-interest are manifest. At the same time, as we have shown above, a positive interest in participating is a prerequisite for an order to function.

An order that is based on explicit rules facilitates social control (6). If the rules are sufficiently clear, there need be no

6. For a discussion of this concept see Janowitz, chap. I.

doubt about the occurrence of infringement. Established rules also normally possess a higher legitimacy than, say, the practice that emerges in a power system.

Explicit and clear rules therefore have the advantage that they can be provided with sanctioning instruments. A notorious problem, however, is that international compromises are often brought about through texts that can be given various interpretations. Even when only the United States and Great Britain negotiated about the future trading order, in a common language and in the middle of a raging war, unanimity could be achieved only by allowing varying interpretations on either side of the Atlantic. When many states participate, with differing languages, cultures, and legal traditions, the difficulties are multiplied exponentially.

The postwar order that has operated so far has benefited from the fact that it was elaborated and established by a small group of countries. These had a common system of cultural values and shared experiences of the problems following the First World War, the Depression, the common effort during the Second World War, and the threat from Communism. Other countries were subsequently allowed to join the established order.

But the order of the postwar period was based also on an accepted hegemony, in the sense that the United States was the self-evident leader at least until the middle of the 1950s. The problem with hegemonic solutions is obviously that they cannot be created. Either a distribution of power exists as an inescapable fact, or else other solutions have to be sought. This may cause apprehensions for the future, as the well-functioning international orders that we know of during the last hundred years have been hegemonic (7).

One advantage of hegemonic solutions is that they solve a number of institutional problems. Existing international organizations are not equipped to deal with the problems that are now constantly cropping up. First and foremost, the international

---

7. Kindleberger, who is an energetic advocate of hegemonic solutions, believes that one reason for the extent of the depression during the thirties was the lack of firm leadership of the world economy because the hegemonic leadership was in the process of being transferred from Great Britain to the United States (see Calleo, pp. 34–5).

organs lack all effective instruments to enforce the rules. As long as the United States was accepted as the world's police force there was a ready-made organization for law and order. Even the industrial countries were forced to submit to a fairly detailed control of their internal concerns (8). The American central bank became the dominant currency institution for the whole Western world. Power was exercised by an existing, functioning administration which was not hampered by lengthy negotiations before necessary measures could be adopted.

The explanation for the stability of the world order during the period 1958–68 was not, however, primarily the unlimited power of the United States. The reason was partly that this power was accepted by other countries, partly that the other OECD countries got what they wanted out of the existing order. Hegemonic solutions can certainly not rest exclusively on a naked exercise of power.

Regional solutions are to be seen as a kind of 'second best' solution. If it is impossible to create a common, global system of rules, it may be possible for a group of countries with sufficiently strong common interests to establish a regional order. This need not be an alternative to a world order. The European Community regards itself primarily as a building-block — in parity with Japan and the United States — in a future international order.

It is not self-evident, however, that it is easier to establish a global order on the basis of regional blocs. There is much to suggest that the established nation state is better able to adapt itself to an international system of rules than regional blocs, which contain within themselves all the problems involved in creating and maintaining a legitimate global order.

The methods listed here for sustaining an international order do not, as we have said, exclude each other. Altruistic behaviour is always a welcome additional factor. A desire to participate for motives of self-interest is a necessary — but probably not sufficient — ingredient. One can never ignore a given power structure. It sets the limits for what is feasible and influences the 'financing' of the public good. Certain clear, internationally

8. See for example Kohr, p. 206.

agreed rules are necessary to promote legitimacy and to intensify the threat of sanctions. An economic world order presupposes a number of co-ordinated mechanisms in order for it to remain integrated — and the mixture may vary between one sphere of activity and another.

A further important factor is obviously general inertia and a lack of alternatives. It is almost always easier to preserve an existing order than to create a new one. In the present situation, for example, the lack of concrete alternatives is evident, although the existing order is subject to severe strains and has been declared by a majority of the countries in the world to be ready for the scrap-heap of history. For the majority of the countries in the world, and especially for the industrial countries, it is vital to avoid chaos at any price. The main strength of the present order — in a situation where no alternative is in sight — is its very existence.

Order or justice

A stable free-trade order means that enterprises and governments can make a reasonable forecast of the future. This boosts not only the total volume of investment but also the degree of risk-taking. In a secure environment risky investments increase in science and technology, as does the willingness to locate production abroad. A functioning free-trade order, in short, promotes an effective international division of labour and thus global economic growth (9).

Stability and growth promote each other. The greater the stability, the more investments and go-ahead research there will be. This leads to higher growth, which in its turn contributes to stability, primarily by enabling all to get a share of a growing cake. That is the beneficent circle. In the vicious one, growing instability hampers economic activity. Growth declines or ceases, and this eventually accentuates the instability.

When the rules function, the costs of uncertainty diminish

9. It is not certain, on the other hand, that international stability increases growth within each of the participating countries. It is theoretically conceivable that certain countries — e.g. countries with high wages and internal stability — may achieve higher growth in a more unstable international order.

for all concerned. Less effort has to be expended on working out alternative investment calculations or on assessing the likely trend of foreign-exchange rates. Less replanning and fewer redispositions have to be undertaken.

This is the inherent value of order expressed in economic terms. The question of justice plays as small a part as in economic science generally. We simply assume that a greater global productive output is better than a smaller one.

But it is precisely the distribution of the global productive output that is the cause of complaints by the developing countries. They claim that the old order has been biased in favour of the established industrial countries. The developing countries have therefore as a group worked out a proposal for a new international economic order (10). One of the main aims of this scheme is to widen the export opportunities of the developing countries by preferential treatment and general liberalization and to increase the income from exports of primary commodities by means of controls. We shall not discuss here whether the developing countries' demands are just or not. Several of the proposals could, in any case, be accommodated within the old order without difficulty, provided that a certain amount of generosity is shown by the industrialized countries.

The problem we are dealing with here relates to the possibility of industrialized and developing countries agreeing on a new world order. Hitherto the developing countries have played a subsidiary role. They were never given the opportunity to influence, or even express their opinion of, the old order. The changes that they have succeeded in bringing about are marginal so far. On the other hand they have been allowed, for example in the field of trade and foreign exchange, to apply the rules very flexibly.

In a future order, however, more developing countries must participate. An agreement with the OPEC states appears to be an increasingly urgent matter for the OECD countries. The so-called newly industrializing countries are becoming ever more important both as markets and as competitors. The necessity of increasing investments in raw-material extraction affects several

10. An account of the developing countries' demands for a new international economic order is given in Anell & Nygren.

countries in Asia, Africa, and Latin America as well as the East European countries.

The problem has sometimes been phrased as if the developing countries were seeking justice while the wealthy countries wish primarily to preserve the existing order (11). There is an obvious kernel of truth in this: it is always the privileged who argue for the maintenance of an order. At the same time it is quite clear that it is primarily a group of developing countries, above all the newly industrializing countries, which benefit from the preservation of the present order, while several industrialized countries see increasing difficulties in a continued adaptation to free trade.

The wealthy industrial countries will set their stamp on the international system of rules during the rest of this century. But the economic world order cannot become hegemonic. The group of developing countries will successively strengthen their ability to influence the rules of the game. The states of the world then face a situation which demands the maintenance of a collectively managed order in which several countries or groups of countries with different cultures, value systems, and interests must collaborate.

11. Ali Mazrui quoted in Bull, p. 77.

II. THE LONG BOOM

And the wind shall say
'Here were decent godless people;
Their only monument the asphalt road
And a thousand lost golf balls'.

T.S. Eliot

Modern bourgeois society ... which has
conjured up such gigantic means of production and exchange, is like the sorcerer
who is no longer able to control the powers
of the nether world whom he has called
up by his spells.

Karl Marx and Friedrich Engels

In a historical perspective, the economic development of the
postwar period up to the depression of the 1970s will be seen
as one long and happy boom. It is during this stable period of
expansion that the wealthy industrial countries establish 'the
old economic order'. Looked at in greater detail, one can
divide this process into three fairly distinct phases. The different conditions applying during each of them clearly influence
the regional spread of trade, terms of trade, international
capital movements, and institutional conditions.

In this chapter I shall first very briefly describe the economic and institutional developments during the three phases (1).

---

1. A somewhat more detailed account of the origin and development of the economic
   order is given in Anell & Nygren, pp. 37ff.

I shall then outline the unique combination of forces that sustained the prolonged boom.

The three phases

The first phase of the prolonged boom extended from the end of the war through 1951. It was dominated by reconstruction in the war-ravaged countries and by the inflation caused by the outbreak of the Korean War.

The United States financed its participation in the Second World War through increased production. All resources were mobilized to build up an enormous productive capacity, which at the end of the war was regarded as too large for the home market. The war effort had introduced the economic policy that finally solved the problems of unemployment, but now a new depression threatened. That was at any rate the 'conventional wisdom' dominating the minds of the decision-makers in Washington at the end of the war. The United States simply had to increase exports in order to be able to provide jobs for the returning soldiers.

Japan and Europe were in need of everything from capital goods to foodstuffs. Crop failures in 1945-6 produced an acute situation in Western Europe. But industry was badly damaged and disorganized. The war-ravaged countries could not pay for the necessary imports with exports of their own.

Under these conditions the scale of transatlantic trade was largely determined by the willingness of the United States to grant credits. Initially the situation was handled tolerably well with bilateral loans — chiefly from the United States and Canada — and through the UN aid programmes. However, the intensification of the cold war which occurred very soon after the end of the war convinced Congress that more long-term and systematic measures were needed. The Marshall Plan started in 1948, and during a four-year period grants and credits amounting to $ 12.5 billion were extended to Western Europe.

The majority of the war-ravaged countries regained their pre-war level of production in both agriculture and industry as early as the end of the forties or the beginning of the fifties. This also applied to the East European countries. However, despite the rapid recovery there remained a fundamental imbalance between the heavily-strained European economies and the technologically-superior productive apparatus of the United States. Trade with the dollar countries remained strictly regulated.

The situation of the developing countries during this phase was dominated by the tremendous rise in the prices of primary commodities. This development was triggered by inadequate productive capacity, was sustained by a continuing boom in the United States, and culminated when the Americans replenished their strategic raw-material reserves in connection with the outbreak of the Korean War.

Foreign investments were of moderate proportion during this period. The economic order still existed more as a matter of intentions than as a tangible reality. The uncertainty in the strategic sphere was underlined by the Berlin blockade and the Prague coup in 1948, and was confirmed by the outbreak of the Korean War in June 1950. In the United States the home market and credit-financed exports had a greater attraction than uncertain foreign investments (2).

It was during this phase that the institutional foundation was laid for the economic order of the postwar period — and it grew out of the experiences of the inter-war period. The aim was to avoid at any cost the problems that led to depression, international collapse — and thus to the recently concluded war. The Americans were firmly resolved to establish a stable order that would open the way to free trade, private capital movements, and a solid monetary system.

The agreements on two of the central organs, the International Monetary Fund (IMF) and the International Bank for Reconstruction and Development (IBRD), were signed while the war was still in progress. Both organizations began their operations on a small scale at the end of the forties.

The first attempt to create a firm system of rules for international trade failed. The regulations for an International Trade

2. During the war net savings in the United States reached enormous figures in private bank accounts. This money created the basis for a marked rise in private consumption. At the same time the state, through grants and credits to other countries, financed an export surplus corresponding to 4 per cent of GNP (Solomon, p. 14).

Organization (ITO) which were signed by the governments of the world at a conference in Havana in 1948 were not accepted by Congress in Washington. Instead a series of bilateral trade negotiations were initiated in Geneva the following year. Thereby the foundation was laid for the General Agreement on Tariffs and Trade (GATT), which eventually developed into the predominant international trade organization. The GATT regulations became the world's first multilateral trade order.

Already after the first GATT negotiations it was clear that a functioning method had been found. There was a growing realization that a development towards progressively lower barriers to international trade had been initiated. This stability, i.e. the possibility of predicting future developments, provided a significant explanation for the expansion in world trade that followed.

IMF, IBRD, and GATT represented the institutional framework for the economic order that had already been planned in detail by the Americans during the war.

The central institution, however, was the American government. During the early postwar period the United States held a predominant position in the Western world in military power, productive capacity, level of technology, and cultural influence. Nothing could be done without American approval. The internal order in developing countries and several West European democracies was guaranteed by Washington, whether this was desired or not. Both IMF and IBRD remained completely subordinate to the American government far into the fifties. It was a unilateral decision in Washington that established that free trade was not to apply to agricultural raw materials. It was an American world order that was created — and it was accepted by the other industrial countries. The developing countries and Eastern bloc states were hardly consulted.

It was, however, only during *the second phase*, 1952-8, that the planned order could be fully realized. It came into effect in stages. If one were to give a precise date at which the 'old' order 'came to fruition' it would be 1958. In that year the majority of industrial countries made their currencies freely convertible against the dollar.

It was during this second phase that some of the basic trends in the international economy became visible. The expansion in world trade was to an increasing extent supported by a rapidly growing exchange of industrial commodities. The most dynamic component in international trade was the internal trade of the OECD countries in manufactured products. The trend was most negative for exports of agricultural and other raw materials from the developing countries.

Table II.1　Growth of world exports at current prices 1950–70 for industrialized, developing, and centrally planned countries (annual percentage increase)

	1950–60	1960–70
Industrialized countries	7.0	10.0
Developing countries	3.0	6.9
Centrally planned countries	10.8	8.7
Whole world	6.4	9.2

Source:　UNCTAD: *Handbook 1976*, p. 25.

The resources of the World Bank increased markedly during the fifties and its activities were directed more and more to the granting of credits for development projects in the developing countries. It was nevertheless still an institution dependent on the good will of Washington and the credits of Wall Street. The Monetary Fund still played a subordinate role as regards the control of developments in the foreign-exchange market. That the planned monetary order could eventually come into effect was above all due to the fact that Japan and the European countries rapidly caught up on the economic and technological lead of the United States. Throughout the fifties productivity increased in Japan and Western Europe at a manifestly more rapid rate than in the American economy.

This development made it possible to bring into being an arrangement with fixed exchange rates and convertibility. International liquidity, however, was still achieved primarily through deficits in the American balance of payments and was thus dependent on the condition of the United States economy. Within GATT the work of eliminating tariffs and other trade barriers continued. The result of the Dillon Round of 1961 reinforced the development towards a stable free-trade order.

Private capital movements increased during the fifties relatively quickly from a modest level. They were due primarily to overseas establishment of American and British enterprises. The book value of foreign investments by American enterprises increased from about $7 billion in 1946 to $25 billion in 1957 and reached $55 billion in 1966. In the latter year American foreign investments still constituted nearly two-thirds of the total book value of the foreign investments of the OECD countries (3). A large part consisted of investments to assure the supply of raw materials. The establishment of transnational corporations overseas in manufacturing industry was aimed primarily at maintaining and extending control of important markets.

The third phase — from the end of the fifties to the beginning of the seventies — was characterized initially by an evident stability in all spheres. From the middle of the 1960s, however, the problems of the monetary order increased, and in 1973 the attempts to force a system of fixed exchange rates on a recalcitrant reality had to be given up for good.

Foreign-exchange crises are often spectacular, prestige-ridden — and infectious. Floating exchange rates, however, did not bring about any fundamental transformation of the economic order. The world's currencies were still freely convertible for current transactions. In other spheres the established order by and large retained its stability during this third phase.

Within GATT the Kennedy Round was carried through during 1962-7, and as a result tariffs may be said to have ceased to be a serious barrier for the industrialized countries' trade in manufactured products. Strategically the situation was also stabilized. The Cuba crisis was too short-lived to affect the economic order — and its solution initiated a development towards greater detente. The two superpowers began to learn the procedures in the ritual of the balance of terror — and there was never any risk of a direct Soviet intervention in Vietnam.

Only in the 1970s did monetary instability spread to other spheres. Among the OECD countries more and more governments began to lose their grip on inflation. Protectionist

3. Rolfe, pp. 205-6.

tendencies which had previously been confined to agricultural commodities and cotton textiles spread to new sectors at the same time as the formal adherence to free-trade principles was reaffirmed.

The basic trends in trade that have been indicated above were reinforced during this phase. Industrial commodities, which constituted well under half of world trade at the beginning of the 1950s, increased their share to 55% in 1960 and to about two-thirds at the beginning of the 1970s. The internal trade of the OECD countries in industrial products constituted about 20% of total world trade at the beginning of the 1950s. By 1960 the figure was around 25% and by 1970 about 33%.

The terms of trade between the prices of primary commodities and industrial products were relatively stable throughout the 1960s.

Protected by the stability of the 1960s, private overseas investments really gathered momentum. American overseas investments increased from a book value of some $ 30 billion at the beginning of the sixties to around $ 80 billion by 1970. However, the increase in West German and Japanese overseas investments was even more rapid. The aggregate book value of all direct investments overseas in 1971 was about $ 165 billions (4).

The stable expansion

During the whole of the prolonged boom — from the end of the 1940s through 1973 — production grew in a rapid and stable manner in all regions of the world. The economic growth of the industrial countries was slightly above 4 per cent during the fifties and close to 5 per cent in the period 1960-73. The rapid 6 per cent annual growth in production by the centrally planned countries during the 1950s fell to 4-5 per cent in the following decade. The average annual growth in GDP of the developing countries was 5-6 per cent (5).

---

4. Wilkins, pp. 329-31; UN: *Multinational Corporations*; UN: *Transnational Corporations*.
5. Including southern Europe.

Table II.2   Economic   growth   1950-76   of   industrialized,
             developing, and centrally planned countries (annual
             percentage)

	1950–1960	1960–1965	1965–1970	1970–1973	1974	1975	1976
Industrial countries	4.1	5.2	4.7	4.6	-0.1	-0.6	4.6
Developing countries	5.0	5.6	5.8	6.0	5.5	5.0	6.4
Centrally planned countries	6.0	4.5	4.3	4.8	6.3	5.4	5.3

Sources: 1950-73 from IBRD: *World Tables*, table 1, except
for the figure for developing countries 1950-60, which is taken
from UNCTAD: *Handbook 1976*, pp. 34–42; 1974-6 for industrialized and developing countries from IBRD: *Annual Report
1978*, and for centrally planned countries from United Nations:
Supplement to World Economic Survey, 1978, p. 106

   The average rate of expansion for the whole world economy
amounted to 5 per cent during the period 1945-73. This growth
was fairly evenly distributed. Notable departures from the average applied mainly to individual countries. Within the OECD
group it was primarily Japan and − during the 1950s − West
Germany which showed a positive divergence, and Great Britain
a negative one. The growth rate of the United States was somewhat lower than in the other industrial countries. Among the
developing countries, the growth rate for southern Asia was
markedly lower than in other regions. This was largely due to
the fact that India's growth rate was lower than that of most
other countries in the Third World.
   This global distribution of a rapid growth in production may
possibly reflect the fact that the postwar period was the first era
of world history in which virtually all the peoples on earth, as
independent nations, established rapid economic growth as

a central political goal (6).

The economic development of the postwar period was also unique in two other respects. The expansion took place at a faster rate than in any comparable previous period and was characterized by manifest stability.

In the case of the developing countries all calculations for earlier periods are extremely uncertain. It is probable, however, that nearly all developing countries achieved a growth rate during the postwar period which was definitely more rapid than ever before, whether they were then colonies or sovereign states (7). In the case of the OECD countries it is quite clear that the rate of growth has increased in comparison with previous periods. The only exception may possibly be the United States, which had a weak development during the 1950s. The majority of OECD countries increased their production during the 1950s and 1960s more than twice as fast as during the period 1870-1913. In Sweden the difference was smaller, mainly because its GDP before the First World War increased at a very rapid rate. The Soviet Union achieved an extraordinarily rapid growth in production in the inter-war period. It is unlikely that any acceleration has taken place during the postwar period.

If one looks at individual countries, several examples can be found of large variations in the rate of expansion from one year to another (8). The overall picture, however, is characterized by an even and steady expansion with weak undulations around a stable, long-term trend. This applies particularly to the European OECD countries and above all during a period from the end of the fifties to the start of the crises in the seventies (see diagram II.1).

6. China must be regarded as the last major country to adopt the prevalent growth ideology.
7. See Anell & Nygren, p. 69.
8. The total production of the United States decreased, partly as a result of a zealous fight against inflation in 1958 and during the first half of 1970. In West Germany the same thing happened, and for the same reason, during the first half of 1963 and from the second half of 1966 to the first half of 1967. But these 'dips' took place at the same time as the total production of the OECD area increased by a healthy 3-4 per cent.

Diagram II.1 Economic growth of the European OECD countries 1951-78 (annual percentage growth)

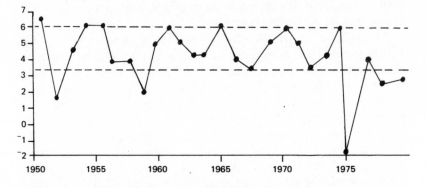

Sources: 1951-60 various annual volumes of *World Economic
          Survey*; 1961-76 *OECD Economic Outlook*, November
          1978.

During the period 1959-73 — the heyday of the 'old' world
order — the growth of the European OECD countries varied
within the interval +3.5% to +6%. The expansion of Canada was
about equally stable, while the fluctuations were somewhat
larger in the Japanese economy (+5% to +15%). The annual rate
of growth for United States' total production varied from 0 to
+6%. Many developing countries also experienced stable growth
during the 1960s, despite large unexpected changes in their
external balances.

The development of world trade was characterized by a marked
stability — and, as in the case of production, was most pronounced during the period from the end of the fifties to the crises of
the 1970s. The growth during 1958-73 on the logarithmic scale
in diagram II.2 is shown as an almost straight line. On the other
hand, as the diagram also shows, there were two minor declines
in the volume of world trade during the 1950s.

During the postwar period world trade increased, as did production, faster than ever before. In terms of volume, international
trade grew during 1953-73 by around 8 per cent a year. This is
almost twice as fast as during the golden age of liberalism in the

Diagram II.2 The volume of world trade 1948-77 (1948 = 100, logarithmic scale)

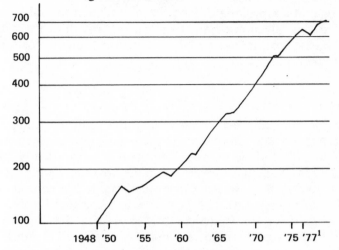

1. The development in 1977 is estimated.
Source: *Barclay's Review*, London, November 1977

middle of the nineteenth century. During the economically and politically stable period before the First World War trade increased by 3-4 per cent.

Table II.3 Growth of the volume of world trade during various periods (annual percentage increase)

Period	Growth
1830–1860	4.2
1873–1913	3.3
1899–1913	3.9
1913–1939	0.9
1953–1973	8.0

Source: Lewis, Arthur

The engines of expansion

It is obvious that there must have been very powerful motive forces behind the prolonged boom. It is important to look more closely at this question since an acceptable growth rate may be a prerequisite for preserving and restoring the present economic world order.

Expansion and stability

Stability implies that all countries play the game according to predetermined rules. The future is then conceived of as certain and predictable for the participating agents. A firm that is considering an investment knows, for example, what tariffs and trade barriers exist in the relevant export markets. It can confine its attention to assessing its own problems and is spared the necessity of speculating on what the effect of political developments may be. Stability of this kind presupposes that all major countries can achieve the adjustments required by the rules of the game. This implies that governments will in the long run accept the outcome of the interplay of market forces. Weak branches are forced to modernize and concentrate on that part of their production that is internationally competitive. In general, the governments must ensure that cost levels develop in roughly the same way as in competitor countries.

This is the ideal picture — the behaviour that was made compulsory by the gold standard at the beginning of the twentieth century and presupposed during the fixed exchange-rate regime in 1958-73.

The ideal has never been fully realized. But during the 1950s and 1960s it is quite clear that a beneficent circle existed in which expansion and stability went hand in hand. During a series of years the production of *all* commodities increased in *all* OECD countries. This provided the necessary scope to achieve structural adjustment and to maintain full employment.

We can also see now which is the chicken and which is the egg. It is the general, stable increase of resources that makes it possible to maintain fixed rules of play. Simultaneously this stable order is a significant factor in explaining the expansion. In a secure environment in which the future can be described by extrapolating given trends, business enterprises can easily assess the conditions for their actions. Investments and overseas establishment become less uncertain, expenditure on research and on new technology becomes more attractive.

When uncertainty and pessimism increased during the 1970s, firms had to raise their risk premiums. Research became more defensive, investments diminished and were increasingly aimed at replacing machines in existing plant; it became more important to retain markets than to capture new ones; planning periods were shortened (9).

And the lower growth during the 1970s does not imply that the structural problems diminished (10). A feeble total expansion is often the result of rapid expansion in certain branches and stagnation or retrogression in others. The latter development is often caused by growing international competition. The main difference between rapid and slow growth is that in the latter case the resources to overcome the problems are more limited.

An important prerequisite for a functioning world order is thus: fair or not, new or old — a world order must rest on a foundation of stability and an acceptable general growth rate. A contributory cause of the prolonged boom is its symbiotic association with a stable order.

Reconstruction and the growth of the consumer society

There is no doubt that growth was largely a response to demand

9. For an account of dwindling and more defensive investments, reduced risk-taking in research, decrease of heavy investments in the Third World, and a declining propensity to invest in shares, see Blackhurst et al.: *Adjustment*, pp. 45-9; Ensor, p. 114, 138, and 177; Blackhurst et al.: *Trade*, pp. 52-9.
10. The Secretariat of the Economic Commission for Europe has attempted to show the dependence of various industries on the total growth in the industrial sector. According to its calculations, which apply to Western Europe, all industries grew when manufacturing industry as a whole increased output by 6% a year, which is what happened during the 1950s and 1960s. With growth rates of 5% a year or less there was a decline first in leather and then also in textiles and clothing. If total growth remained at 3%, leather declined by 4%, clothing and footwear by 2% and textiles by 0.9%. Then the growth rate of the industry producing transport equipment also remained at 1% a year. (*Structure and Change in European Industry*, p. 28.)

until well into the 1960s. The self-evident needs of reconstruction were superseded by the growth of the consumer society — symbolized by the explosive expansion of motoring with its revolutionizing structural effects. This demand, chiefly generated within the OECD countries, was boosted to an increasing extent towards the end of the 1960s by an uncertain and credit-financed demand from the rest of the world.

The need for housing, capital equipment, and consumer goods in the war-ravaged countries was obvious. All resources were mobilized for the work of reconstruction. In the United States and other countries with an intact industry the available capacity was utilized to meet the needs dammed up during the war and for exports to serve reconstruction abroad. At the same time the developing countries were able to increase imports rapidly due to good revenues from exports of primary commodities. Unemployment in the OECD countries was reduced to a lower level than ever before. It is presumably wrong to say that governments adopted the policy of full employment. It was reality that showed that this goal could be realized.

The housebuilding programmes which were initiated in Europe and Japan (11) during the forties and fifties stagnated — often at a high level — during the 1960s. Apart from reconstruction the increased demands on housing standards, changing family structures, and a growing population helped to sustain the expansion. Only very great changes of social structure can again make the housing sector an engine of growth in the economy. There are several reasons, however — including reduced mobility in the labour market, and the rise in housing costs — why such a develop-

---

11. The United States had a manifestly lower growth rate than the other OECD countries throughout the postwar period, but particularly during the fifties. There were several reasons for this. Washington paid a price determined by security policy in order quickly to activate economic growth in Japan and Western Europe. It was the Americans who almost entirely bore the brunt of the adjustment costs when German and Japanese enterprises re-established their previous positions in the world market. Concurrently with the recovery and the more rapid rise in productivity in the other OECD countries, the dollar exchange rate became increasingly unrealistic and restrictive to competition — but its role as a reserve currency made adjustment more difficult. The problem of being in the lead, both as a consumer society and with regard to technology, was felt by the Americans when private consumption rose more quickly in other countries, which furthermore copied American production methods in order to satisfy this demand.

ment is less likely to occur. In several countries, for example France, Italy, the Netherlands, Great Britain, West Germany, Denmark, and Sweden, the number of completed housing units has declined greatly during the 1970s.

The reconstruction phase was superseded in the European OECD countries during the 1950s by the consumer society. A large number of commodities previously reserved for an affluent minority became available to the middle and working classes, through industrial mass-production and rising real wages. It was during the period 1950-70 that motoring made a serious break-through in Western Europe.

During the period 1953-65 the number of private cars quad-rupled in Sweden, Belgium, and France. Among the European OECD countries, only Great Britain had a lower rate of increase. Car ownership among the Dutch multiplied sixfold, that of the West Germans eightfold, and in Italy the number of private cars multiplied ninefold. In North America, which already had a relatively high car density, the figure merely doubled from 1953 to 1965, while the number of cars in Japan multiplied twentyfold. This development of automobilism led to revolutionary changes in the infrastructure of society and in people's life patterns. Automobilism generated a corollary demand in a number of fields and necessitated enormous public investments. The number of private cars continued to increase even after the middle of the 1960s, but the growth now proceeded at a distinctly slower rate.

Consumer capital goods were also among the expansive pro-ducts during this period. Homes turned into small factories for production of an ever-increasing amount of goods and services (12).

The expansion of private consumption during the 1950s was so great that the loss of demand from the developing countries was hardly noticed. The Third World's imports from the OECD area increased only 3% a year at current prices during this decade.

From the middle of the 1960s, however, it is evident that the consumption of consumer capital goods increased at a decidedly

---

12. A person working at home now draws upon greater machine investments than an industrial worker before the First World War (Young & Willmott, p. 98).

slower rate than before in the OECD countries of Western and Northern Europe.

In the wealthier OECD countries both car ownership and the use of 'necessary' consumer capital goods are now close to a probable saturation level. In the United States the number of cars is close to the limit that is generally regarded as the absolute ceiling — 500 cars per 1000 inhabitants. In Europe and Japan there is still some leeway, but it is quite obvious that the increase, up to a probable stagnation, will occur at a fairly moderate pace. It is not likely that the demand for the above-mentioned products in future will become an engine of growth in the economy.

A slackening of demand for traditional consumer goods also leads to a qualitative change. There is now genuine uncertainty about the future development of demand for several of the traditional products — and the coming 'new' products are as always difficult to predict. The European countries have caught up with the United States — there is no longer a model of the future.

Increased uncertainty about the direction of demand leads to greater cautiousness, inefficient utilization of capacity, and lower growth. Simultaneously several developing countries have reached a level where they can copy the European postwar model — to imitate the tested technology of other countries in order to satisfy a rapidly growing and easily predictable demand (13).

Technological renewal and gains in productivity

By technological development we mean in the sequel chiefly the introduction of more effective mechanical equipment, new and cheaper products, and improved production methods in industry. This definition thus embraces both the major advances typified by integrated circuits and semiconductors and the continuous day-by-day improvement that has taken place since the Industrial Revolution. Both kinds of technological development are

13. All available forecasts, e.g. for the car industry, indicate that demand in the developing countries is increasing 5–7 times faster than in the industrialized countries (Yamazaki).

about equally significant for the economic development of the postwar period (14).

Another important cause of the increase in productivity is that labour power moves from low-productivity sectors — above all agriculture — to branches of industry with high productivity. This is an important explanation both of the rapid growth rate in Japan and Western Europe and of the somewhat lower rate in the United States. During the ten-year period 1963-73, 12 million people left agriculture in Western Europe and Japan compared with only 1.5 million in the United States. But the gains from this occupational change are now about to go into reverse. During the fifties there was still a net increase in the number of highly productive industrial jobs. Since the mid-1960s industrial employment has stagnated — at least in the wealthier OECD countries in Europe. The expansion is now taking place in the private and public service sector, where the average productivity is lower.

The simplest and probably the most common way of increasing productivity through technological renewal is that firms acquire a technology that has been developed and tested by those who are at the forefront of research. This is what happened during the postwar period. The business enterprises in Western Europe and Japan successively copied the superior technology of the Americans. Productivity in Europe and Japan increased during the period 1950-70 markedly faster than in the United States (15). Thereby the technological gap was closed between Western Europe and Japan, on the one hand, and the United States on the other. The fact that productivity in the American economy is still higher than in the European market economies is chiefly due to economies of scale (16). The simple way of increasing productivity — by copying what others have developed — is no longer open to the wealthy OECD countries.

The rapid technological development in Western Europe coincides with the prolonged boom. This involves continuous creation of new jobs to replace those that disappear as a

14. Freeman, p. 69.
15. Ensor, p. 23.
16. Pratten, p. 60.

result of rationalization. The new jobs are often in the same enterprise or industry. The trade unions can therefore for a long time adopt a decidedly positive attitude to technological development. By and large it means that their members get higher wages and that inflation is kept in check.

The lower rate of growth that characterized the development during the 1970s led to increased resistance to structural change. The new jobs that were to replace the old ones were not numerous enough and those created were often not accessible to the people who lost their jobs. The gap increased between the knowledge possessed by the unemployed and the skills required for the new jobs. For firms there was a dramatic rise in the cost of retraining technicians and engineers to make them ready for a new technological generation, particularly in the electronics industry. With a low average growth, whole industries suffered a decline and firms were forced into liquidation. To change employment, if that was at all possible, would require both retraining and migration.

We can thus establish that
— the earlier gains when people moved from agriculture to industry have changed into their opposite. It is now primarily the low productivity and — as I shall later demonstrate — problem-ridden service sector that is growing
— the simple source of technological renewal — to copy a technologically superior economy — has largely been exhausted for the wealthy European OECD countries and Japan
— the climate for technological restructuring depends directly on whether the growth-stability circle is vicious or beneficent. If the threats to jobs continue to grow, an increasing resistance will make technological restructuring more difficult.

On the other hand we do not know — and we may as well admit it — whether technological and scientific innovations will in future permit a faster or slower increase in productivity. Economists who ought to be qualified to answer the question have reached totally divergent conclusions. My own view is that the technological advances already achieved and the new products and processes which have been tested on a small scale make it certain that an extraordinarily rapid growth in productivity is technically feasible during the remainder of this century. Whether and, if so, how it can be achieved is a considerably more difficult question, to which I shall return.

Keynesian policy and the public sector

Keynesian policy did not become established as applied theory until after the war, partly because it had had to be practised and found to be successful during the war. This theory provides an explanation for the fact that an economy can reach equilibrium when available resources are not fully utilized, something which was ruled out as impossible before Keynes. The productive capacity is not utilized to satisfy existing needs because the effective demand is and/or is expected to be too low. Previously the prescription of economists for such situations had been to lower wages so that investors could again obtain a sufficient return on their capital. Keynes's objection to this view was based on the fact that the problem is insufficient demand and this is only aggravated if wages are lowered. Instead the government should intervene with stimulative measures — e.g. investment programmes in the public sector — which are financed through loans. In this way an economic expansion is achieved so that a new equilibrium is reached at a higher level.

It is, however, important to remember that there are two essential preconditions for the Keynesian policy. In the first place it assumes a generally low utilization of capacity. This makes it possible to increase production in all industries. Secondly, the theory only applies to a closed economy.

If, instead, we have a situation in which idle capacity exists in certain industries — e.g. shipyards, steelworks, and the pulp industry — and the reason is that these industries find it difficult to compete with foreign countries, then the situation is quite different. A general upsurge of demand will in that case lead, on the one hand, to inflation, because the industries that already utilize their resources fully can raise their prices, and on the other to a weaker balance of payments on current account, because imports will increase. The only positive effect is that industries that are internationally competitive will be stimulated to extend their capacity. As a solution for short-term problems, however, the Keynesian policy has become a very blunt instrument in small, open market economies with structural problems.

In large countries like the United States and Japan the share of imports in total consumption remains low in the case of industrial commodities — well below 10 per cent. Only in the case of clothing and metals is it higher. Even if the so-called marginal import propensity may be considerably above the average, the leakages are small enough to make a policy of demand stimulation a feasible option in these two countries. Even for Great Britain the situation is different. In 1975 34 per cent of the total consumption of industrial commodities was made up of imports compared to 17 per cent fifteen years earlier. For individual EEC countries, as well as for smaller industrial countries, the import share is of the same size or even larger.

This means, among other things, that policies of demand stimulation must be co-ordinated among the OECD countries in order to become effective. It must be possible to compensate for the increased imports generated by the stimulation of demand in *one* country by increasing exports to other countries in order that a balance of external payments may be maintained.

The Keynesian theory provided governments with an instrument that functioned, or at least was considered to function (which is almost as important) during the early postwar period. This contributed to the rapid growth and full employment. In recent years a number of problems have gradually grown in intensity and reduced the effectiveness of the instrument. The majority of OECD countries have considerable structural problems and the competition from the newly industrializing countries will undoubtedly aggravate them. The new interdependence of the industrialized countries has increased the leakages in general demand stimulation.

This would in itself be sufficient to justify talking of a crisis of economic policy. But for orthodox Keynesians there is a solution, namely internationally co-ordinated demand management. A more fundamental problem is that the very theory of the policy that has hitherto been applied and been thought to function has been called into question. In the United States 'monetarists' and 'non-monetarists' succeed each other as presidential advisers, with widely divergent opinions as to what policies are reasonable and feasible (17). We have got to a place where there is genuine uncertainty as to whether traditional measures of economic policy will work and what a sensible economic policy should look like (18).

The most important effect of the Keynesian revolution, I would maintain, does not relate to the theory of a policy of full employment but to the role of the state in general. Up to the Second World War, virtually all economists agreed that state interventions in the economy were an evil. Keynes managed to convince a few people to the contrary, but it took a depression, a world war, a massive reconstruction effort, and a critical strategic situation to win over the majority. As from the postwar period, state intervention is regarded as legitimate, necessary, and desirable. In this way the science of political economy has legitimized the expansion of the public sector, which is one of the most significant and most characteristic features of the economic expansion during the postwar period — and an important part of the explanation of the long boom.

In all OECD countries the public sector has laid claim to a greatly increased share of total resources. On average the share of the public sector increased during the period 1955-76 from 28 to 42 per cent. The smallest increase took place in France, from 33 to 43 per cent. This is partly due to the fact that the share was already very high at the beginning of the period. The public sector in the United States was relatively less extensive than the average. The increase from 26 to 35 per cent was, however, relatively rapid. Sweden has the most extensive public sector. Most remarkable, though, is the increase from, on average, 17 per cent in 1955-7 to 52 per cent in the period 1974-6. Those parts of the public sector which have increased most rapidly in virtually all countries are education and social welfare.

Later on I will show (chap. V) that even if the present public sector is maintained, this will entail fundamental problems. A

17.An authoritative account of the conflict between monetarists and non-monetarists — two inappropriate but unfortunately accepted epithets — is to be found in Gordon & Pelkmans, pp. 28-39.
18.See also Blackhurst et al.: *Adjustment*, pp. 1-4, and Shonfield, on the theoretical crisis of macroeconomics.

continued rapid expansion along the lines adopted so far is virtually out of the question. The public sector will not be an engine of growth in future.

III. THE CRISIS

The spring of the world
Will soon have uncoiled,
Now is its ultimate hour.
So mark well my word:
To nought have we toiled,
All things are drained now of power.

Lars Wivallius (1605-69)

Rien

Note in the diary of Louis XVI
for 14 July 1789

The deep recession that began in the OECD countries in 1973 has been interpreted in various ways — from the optimistic hope of the McCracken report that the problems can be solved with more intelligent politicians to the confirmation that all doomsday prophecies are coming true. I shall now first outline very briefly the course of the crisis and then discuss its causes.

Background and course

At the end of the 1960s inflation rose noticeably in the majority of OECD countries. This necessitated a restrictive policy which held back economic growth in 1970-1 in both North America and Western Europe. A shift to a policy of greater demand stimulation in 1971-2 occurred at the same time as the world economy entered a very expansive phase. Simultaneously the money supply increased substantially.

49

The result of this was that almost all the OECD countries simultaneously experienced an intensive boom in 1972-3. On an annual basis output increased in the seven leading industrial countries by 8 per cent during the first six months of 1973. Prices soared from the end of 1971. Factors contributing to this were a generally high demand and the above-mentioned increase in liquidity, but also structural problems in several industries. Feeble growth of investment in previous years gave rise to a pronounced shortage of several important industrial inputs. Inadequate grain harvest in several regions and reduced fishing catches off the west coast of Latin America caused food prices to rocket.

Inflation forced governments to pursue tighter economic policies. The effects of this began to emerge at the same time as the OECD countries were hit by the quadrupled oil prices of the OPEC states — a 'tax' corresponding to around 2 per cent of the total output of the wealthy countries. The recession thus became both synchronized and unusually profound.

The authors of the McCracken report are thus right when they note that the chief cause of the crisis of 1974-5 'was an unusual bunching of unfortunate disturbances' (1). It is equally clear that the crisis deepened as a result of 'some avoidable errors in economic policy'.

'Harmonization' during the boom was succeeded by an almost total lack of co-ordination among the OECD countries during the crisis, manifested, for instance, in a very uneven distribution of deficits in the balances of current account. In 1975, while the United States and West Germany had a combined surplus of $22.5 billion, Japan and France were in balance and the other OECD countries showed a total deficit of almost $40 billion. Overall, the volume of industrial output in the OECD countries

---

1. *Towards Full Employment*, p. 14. Whether it is also true to assert that this unfortunate combination 'will probably not be repeated to the same extent' (p. 14) we shall discuss below. See also the analysis of the electoral-economic cycle in Tufte. One reason for 'the appearance of economic interdependence . . . may simply be the internationalization of the US electoral-economic cycle' (p. 69). It seems clear that the Nixon administration created a booming economy from the end of 1971 in order to produce a favourable climate for the 1972 elections (pp. 45-55).

diminished by 10 per cent from July 1974 to April 1975 and the volume of intra-OECD trade fell by 13 per cent.

The most troublesome legacies of the crisis are a continuing high inflation and extensive unemployment. The slump of 1974-5 caused the number of unemployed people in the OECD countries to rise from 8-9 million to over 15 million. At the beginning of 1977 the IMF estimated unemployment at 16.3 million people in the industrialized countries, about 5.5 per cent of the labour force. In 1980 the unemployment rate is estimated at 6 per cent, and the forecast of the IMF is that the situation will get worse (2).

International inflation was practically negligible throughout the 1960s, about 1.5 per cent a year. The boom of 1972-3 led to a violent international inflation. In connection with the recession of 1974-5 inflation was considerably reduced both internationally and nationally, though without returning to levels that were regarded as acceptable in the OECD countries in the mid-1960s.

During 1975 a considerable economic recovery took place in the majority of OECD countries, and output continued to increase during 1976-9. Growth was, however, clearly lower than during the 1960s and was unable to alleviate unemployment. The crisis acquired an ever more classical character. Large unsatisfied demands existed at the same time as the existing productive capacity was only partially utilized.

Cause and significance

The crisis during the 1970s can be, and has been, explained as both a cyclical and a structural phenomenon. My own understanding is roughly this. The timing of the crisis can be satisfactorily explained by traditional business-cycle theory (3). But the decline of production coincided with and intensified a number of structural problems that had long been on their way to the surface.

The crisis of the seventies was not exclusively or even mainly an economic crisis. I shall, however, come back to the political

2.   *IMF Survey*, 9 January 1978. *World Economic Outlook*, p. 14.
3.   The slump in 1973-4 was also predicted by several economic analysts. See for example *The Economist*, 23 June 1973.

and cultural aspects of the problems of the welfare states. In this
section attention is therefore concentrated on economic characteristics.

The resistance of the OECD countries to structural changes
became evident very early, in spite of all the declarations in
favour of free trade. Agriculture was kept outside the GATT
system as a totally protected sector. Early low-wage competition
was countered in 1962 by the cotton textile agreement, backed
up by 'voluntary' trade restrictions. The prolonged and stable
boom of 1958-73 provided resources with which to 'subsidize
away' disagreeable structural adjustment. The regional policies
that emerged during the 1960s were both an expression of new
value-patterns and a new name for government subsidies to non-
competitive industries. In the majority of OECD countries state
subsidies calculated in proportion to GNP started to increase
from the middle of the 1960s (4). Mobility in the labour market
decreased, for economic as well as other reasons. These tendencies
– which all undermined the expansive forces in and automatic
adjustment capacity of the economies – slowly increased in
strength throughout the sixties.

Concurrently demand gradually fell off for a range of heavy
consumer capital goods, and in some cases completely stagnated.
This did not only mean that the pressure of demand was subdued.
It has also created a growing uncertainty as to what products
will be demanded in the future. On the production side, the two
simple methods of increasing productivity had been exhausted.
There was no longer a superior North American technology to
copy. Instead the OECD countries were threatened 'from behind'
by a number of newly industrializing countries. The gains derived
from people moving out of agriculture into the factories of the
cities remained. But they were more than eaten up by the fact
that new jobs were now created in the 'low-productivity' service
sector. All of this pointed towards a likely reduction in growth
even before the crisis.

The first acute crisis in the international economic order
related to the monetary system. And from this source inflation
and instability spread to other spheres.

4.   Blackhurst et al.: *Trade Liberalization*, p. 46.

The nucleus of the old monetary system was the American dollar and its fixed relation to gold. For 35 dollars central banks could buy one ounce of fine gold. A stable dollar in a system of fixed exchange rates imposed a certain discipline on the other currencies. Inflation had to be reduced to a level that was compatible with the given exchange rate. The American inflation became normative and this was an important reason why the rise in the international price level was negligible during most of the 1960s.

From the middle of the 1960s the administration in Washington tried to finance the Vietnam War parallel with social reforms simply by printing more money. The result was that the international monetary system collapsed. When the system of fixed exchange rates eventually had to be abandoned it became evident that a government has the freedom to choose not only an exchange rate but also a rate of inflation.

The recession of 1974-5 was preceded by a large increase in the money supply. Inflation gathered momentum and there was now no longer any international order to restrain it.

We can thus see that the economic order — both nationally and internationally — was already subject to serious stresses when the first so-called oil crisis occurred in 1973-4. The effect of the recession was above all to make at once visible and acute all the structural problems that had slowly been surfacing.

As early as the end of the 1960s a gap arose between potential and actual output. Not even during the intensive and synchronized boom that preceded the oil crisis was this gap closed. Part of the productive apparatus that was kept alive with state subsidies was not needed even during the peak of the business cycle (5).

These structural problems were drastically aggravated by the crisis. The world shipping industry was already in difficulties at the beginning of the 1970s. Japan, which employed half of the world's bulk tonnage during the 1960s, had 'asianized' its trade and shortened the transport distances considerably (6). Another reason was that the transport requirements of the United States for the Vietnam War had diminished.

5.   See Herin, p. 15.
6.   Bolang, p. 107.

Diagram III.1 Actual and potential GNP of the OECD countries
(1963 prices and exchange rates)

– – – – – – – potential GNP

———————— actual GNP

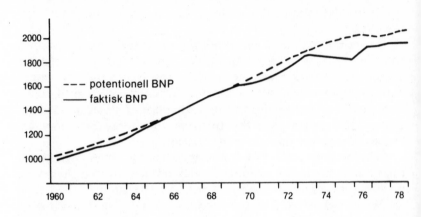

Source: Herin

Due to the oil crisis in 1973 a quarter of the world's tanker
and bulk tonnage became redundant overnight. Shipyards were
entirely deprived of new orders for that type of ship and reduced
their steel purchases. From the steel industry the crisis passed
on to the mining sector (7).

Trade problems were also aggravated by the crisis. The cotton
textile agreement was replaced by the more rigorous and inclusive
Multifibre Agreement, which has already had a marked effect in
restricting trade (8). In 1976 the EEC introduced a scheme
resembling agricultural controls, in order to protect its steel
producers. The United States followed the EEC's example in the
matter of steel and also negotiated restrictions on the importa-
tion of such things as TV sets and footwear. The disturbances of

7. *Teknik och industristruktur*, p. 19.
8. An excellent short account of the Multifibre Agreement is given in *World Trade
and the International Economy*, pp. 9ff.

the external balances caused by the rising cost of oil imports 'forced' a number of industrialized countries to make use of their legislation in the commercial sphere, for example with regard to anti-dumping measures, with a clearly restrictive aim. The GATT Secretariat has calculated that the trade restrictions introduced during 1975-6 affect 3-5 per cent of world trade (9).

The crisis revealed a number of structural weaknesses both in the economies of the OECD countries and in the international system — and it led to a vast number of new supportive measures for ailing industries. State subsidies to industries affected by the crisis increased greatly. The financing was done largely by means of the banknote-printing presses. In all OECD countries the crisis led to rapidly increasing fiscal deficits in the consolidated public sector (10). This confirmed what the general public had already begun to suspect and to accommodate itself to, namely that governments were no longer able to combat inflation (11).

Nor does there seem to be an effective cure for the growing unemployment. Those OECD countries that could have pursued an expansive policy during the crisis did not do so because they gave priority to anti-inflation policies. This 'forcibly transferred' the deficits to those countries that wished to pursue an expansive policy but were now unable to do so because their external balance was weakened. In the absence of international co-ordination the Keynesian policy no longer functioned.

'Oil crisis' is a misleading term if one looks to the purely economic effects. Quadrupled oil prices meant a 'taxation' of the OECD countries which gave an additional impetus to the recession but definitely did not cause it.

It is true of course that the era of cheap energy has come to an end. Still the oil crisis was and is above all psychological. In a narrow economic sense the consequences of the price rise stem mainly from the suddenness of the change and not from its magnitude. In a wider sense, however, the oil crisis generated an uncertainty throughout the industrialized world and indirectly

9. *New York Times*, 23 September 1977. With regard to growing protectionism see also United Nations: *Transnational Corporations*, pp. 16ff; *World Development Report 1978*, pp. 14-16; Keesing, p. 80; and Blackhurst: *Trade*, p. 44.
10. See below, pp. 102-103.
11. Van Cleveland & Huertas, p. 112.

affected every single major investment decision that has been made since the autumn of 1973. Is it reasonable to continue to depend on oil? What is the price likely to be in ten or twenty years' time? Will there even be any oil available? How stable is the situation in Saudi Arabia? No enterprise is unaffected by the answers to these questions — and developments since the crisis have not made it any easier to answer them.

The oil crisis made it brutally clear that the world order is not a matter that is determined by Washington in consultation with a few selected governments. Future economic orders must be more broadly based. And this is a step into the unknown. The economic orders that have functioned during the last hundred and fifty years have been hegemonic. Now there is no longer an accepted power structure as a basis.

The old beneficent circle where rapid growth generated a stable order has been progressively weakened since the end of the 1960s. With the oil crisis it was transformed into its opposite. From the end of the fifties through 1973, output increased in the seven leading industrial countries by over 5 per cent. From 1973 and throughout the rest of the seventies GDP grew at only half that rate. This did not provide governments with sufficient room to manoeuvre to work out a rational long-term policy. A growth of 2.5 per cent was not sufficient to absorb the annual increase in the labour force (12) and the already high unemployment continued to rise. Governments lacked the power to distribute resources *within* the given frameworks. The result was an uncontrolled inflation that threatened both national and international order.

At the same time uncertainty increased as to how the traditional instruments of economic policy were functioning. Was the failure of stabilization policies due to the fact that economies no longer function as expected, or was there something wrong with the theory? Could an increase in the money volume create more jobs or would it *only* lead to a renewed acceleration of inflation? This genuine uncertainty made it practically impossible to reach agreement on an internationally co-ordinated policy of stabilization. Not even in theory were there any sound and simple

12.*Inflation and Unemployment*, p. 16.

solutions. The practice of the sixties was not relevant to the problems of the seventies. This is part of the significance of the crisis that we carry with us unresolved into the eighties.

IV. THE INTERNATIONALIZATION OF THE WORLD ECONOMY

> Little by little the pimps have taken over the world. They don't do anything, they don't make anything — they just stand there and take their cut.
>
> *Jean Giraudoux*

> Property, its undisturbed maintenance and transmission, has created the social order and all its laws. It is the basis of power and the objective of its exercise. It is therefore natural to trace the path of property in order to indicate the path of power.
>
> *Honoré de Balzac*

In this chapter I shall describe the continuously increasing interdependence that characterizes the economic development during the postwar period. The aspects which I have chosen to highlight are the international trade in industrial products, the relations between 'new' and 'old' industrial countries, and the operations of the transnational corporations in an internationalized yet simultaneously unstable world economy. First, however, I shall indicate why there is cause to speak of a new form of international economic interdependence.

The new interdependence

All periods of stability in the world economy give rise to internationalization in the sense that international trade, capital transfers between countries and overseas investments tend to increase more rapidly than total production. The enterprises that are market leaders — and therefore pace-setters — have a global outlook. Threatening competition may come from many quarters and the productive factors of labour, agricultural land, and raw materials are only to a limited extent mobile. When the stability of the world economy is acceptable, enterprises will venture to acquire a stake in capital-intensive mining investments and low-wage industries in otherwise risky countries. The development that has occurred during the postwar period is thus a natural outcome of the stability that existed — and it is no coincidence that internationalization proceeded at a particularly rapid pace during 'the golden sixties.'

During virtually the whole of the postwar period trade has increased more rapidly than production — and international capital movements have grown even faster since the 1950s. From the beginning of the 1950s until the mid-1960s international trade grew by around 130 per cent compared with an increase of about 90 per cent for world GDP. This tendency was even more marked during the stable heyday of the old world order from 1960 to 1973. During that period total production increased by 100 per cent, against 180 per cent for trade. The process of internationalization was particularly evident in the industrial sphere. From 1953 to 1965 trade in manufactured products increased twice as fast as industrial production; during the period 1960-74 the growth was 270 and 110 per cent respectively. The book value of foreign private investments of the OECD countries would seem to have amounted to about 3-4 per cent of their total GDP at the beginning of the fifties. At the beginning of the 1970s these investments amounted to around 8-10 per cent.

The figures at this aggregated level do not indicate a uniquely new situation. Trade and capital movements reached the same degree of internationalization as early as the end of the nineteenth century and above all during the long stable period of expansion preceding the First World War. However, the internationalization that took place at that time was largely an illusion, as Charles Cooper has pointed out (1). Large areas of the economy were

1. Cooper, p. 152.

then naturally protected from international competition. Breweries, brickworks, and bakeries supplied local markets. The 'clothing industry' still consisted of local tailors. International freight rates were too high for the furniture industry to engage in international trade. Agriculture, fishing, and handicrafts were not yet integrated even on the national level. World market prices had been established only for a few products — mainly produce of non-European origin such as coffee, sugar, and spices. For many products there was not even a uniform national price. Not until the 1870s did railways make it possible to do what Jules Verne had prophesied — to travel around the world in only eighty days (2). News media had not yet made the general public aware of life styles, culture, and living standards in other countries. Even during the inter-war period the social sciences were still permeated by racist notions about the inhabitants of the colonies. A British prime minister could say in 1938 that his country did not intend to go to war because of 'a quarrel in a faraway country between people of whom we know nothing' (3).

Today the world is an economic unit in quite a different fashion. There is every reason to speak of a new form of interdependence. Transport costs have been reduced so drastically that almost the whole commodity market — the only major exception being some parts of food production — is subject to international competition. Commodities from twenty-one countries may be found in an ordinary market-place in a medium-sized Swedish town (see map).

All engineering products contain components from a large number of different countries. Enterprises have developed a technique for administering and organizing production at a global level. Tariffs have almost ceased to be barriers to trade. During the 1950s genuine American jeans were almost as desirable in Scandinavia as they are today in Eastern Europe. Now waves of fashion and life styles spread among the young generation around the world in a matter of months through films and TV. The Rothschild family — ever since they were

2. Hobsbawm, p. 52. See further pp. 48–50 on the rapid internationalization of the world economy during the nineteenth century.
3. *The Times History of Our Times*, p. 45.

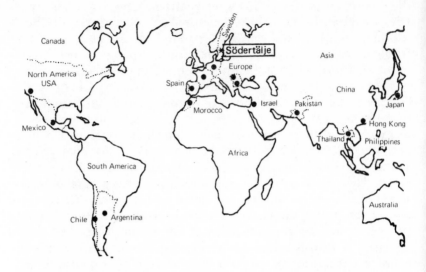

*The black dots on the map show countries of origin for com-
modities on sale in the Södertälje market-place on the last
Saturday in May 1979. They come from all over the world:
wooden clogs from Vollsjö (in Sweden), grapes from Argentina,
tomatoes from Rumania, cauliflower from Brittany, aubergines
from Israel, knick-knacks from Italy, blouses from Pakistan,
dresses from Thailand, flowers from Brunnsang (in Sweden).*

the first to learn the outcome of the battle of Waterloo — built
up their fortune throughout the nineteenth century partly by
developing the fastest and most reliable information system in
the world. Today thousands of bank offices all over the world
are informed about changes in important exchange rates within
a few seconds. People all over the world are instantly informed
about the same major events through news agencies, newspapers,
radio and TV. What John Stuart Mill wrote in 1859 is actually
almost true today — the global upper class live in a world where
people 'read the same things, listen to the same things, see the
same things, go to the same places. . . .' (4). Capital movements

4. Mill, *On Liberty*, quoted in Kumar, p. 93.

have not only reached a massive scale — they have become truly international, in the sense that several capital markets have been established beyond the control of governments (5).

In a growing number of spheres national policies are becoming dependent on conditions in the rest of the world. Taxation policy must be adapted to the trade system. When scientists and business managers can move to other countries, tax policies acquire an international dimension. The education system must provide increased knowledge of 'the world without Verona's walls'. In order to give demand policies sufficient impact they must be coordinated with measures in other countries.

The new interdependence that has evolved during the postwar period thus differs from the internationalization during earlier periods, above all in its qualitative aspects. The international system is more integrated, changes take place faster and affect increasing numbers of people. The international economy is a unified organism. The food crisis of 1974-5 and the uncertain oil situation are the most critical but by no means the only examples of international relationships of dependence that are qualitatively new.

The globalization of the industrial sector

In all the OECD countries manufacturing industry's share of GDP and of total employment has diminished during the last fifteen to twenty years. In the mid-1970s the output of manufacturing industry accounted for less than 30 per cent of total output in the OECD countries.

Yet it is in the industrial sector, and above all in manufacturing industry, that we must look for the important causes of economic expansion and structural change. It is manufacturing industry that introduces the new technology and supplies the new products, that determines international competitiveness and thus the conditions for the process of internationalization.

This section will primarily be devoted to trade in industrial goods; and in particular to the causes of the rapid increase in the so-called intra-industry trade of the OECD countries. First,

5. This aspect of internationalization has been analysed in detail by Engellau & Nygren.

however, we should indicate the important change that has occurred with regard to the location of world industrial production.

The location of industrial production

Within the OECD bloc definite shifts have taken place during the postwar period with regard to relative shares of world industrial output. The most drastic case is the rapid evolution of Japan to a position as one of the leading industrial nations. Japan's share of the total industrial output of the market economies was 4.2 per cent before the war. That position was regained by the Japanese as early as 1960. During the period up to 1973 Japan's share increased to over 10 per cent. West Germany had also regained its pre-war position — 9-10 per cent — by 1960 and increased its share to 14 per cent from 1960 to 1973. These two countries, together with France and Italy, increased their joint share of the industrial output of the market economies by about 22 percentage points from 1950 to 1973. The major losers were the United States, whose share was almost halved from 1950 to 1973, and Great Britain. It was, as I have pointed out above, the domestic industry of the United States that bore the brunt of the burden in connection with the return to more normal conditions in the world economy. The Japanese expansion in particular was absorbed to a notably large degree by the American market.

For several reasons the industrial output of the centrally planned countries is difficult to compare with that of the market economies. The total output in centrally planned countries is reckoned to have been about $ 970 billion in 1973 (6). If industry is assumed to represent 45 per cent of GDP, industrial output would be around $ 435 billion, i.e. almost 30 per cent of the whole world's industrial output, which tallies fairly well with the estimates that have been made by leading analysts of the Eastern bloc economies and by UNIDO (7).

According to UN statistics, industrial output in the centrally

6. *World Trade and Output.*
7. Knirsch, Peter, in: *From Marshall Plan to Global Interdependence*, p. 147. UNIDO's figures for 1975 are 63.7 per cent for developed market economies, 27.7 per cent for centrally planned economies, and 8.6 per cent for developing countries (UNIDO, 1979, p. 34).

Table IV.1 Percentage share of various countries or groups of countries in the total industrial output of the market economies 1938-73.

	1938	1950	1960	1973
United States	35.7	51.2	43.8	29.8
Great Britain	11.1	8.9	7.5	4.8
West Germany	10.6	5.8	9.1	14.1
France	6.2	4.3	4.9	7.5
Italy	2.8	2.0	2.9	3.6
All industrialized countries	–	(90-91)	89.5	88.7
All developing countries (incl. Turkey and Yugoslavia)	–	(9-10)	(10.5)	11.3

Sources: 1938-60 *World Economic Survey 1961*; 1973 calculations based on *IBRD World Tables 1976, World Bank Atlas 1975,* and *World Trade and Output.* Figures in parentheses are estimated. The comparison between 1938-60 and 1973 is uncertain.

planned countries has increased at a definitely faster rate than in the rest of the world throughout the postwar period. With the aid of the UN's index series one can calculate the distribution of industrial output in 1960. A tentative estimate of the distribution of the world's industrial output between industrialized, developing, and centrally planned countries in the years 1960 and 1973 would thus appear as follows:

Table IV.2 World industrial output by region 1960 and 1973

	Output value 1973 $ billions	Percentage 1960	Percentage 1973
Industrialized countries	957	70.6	63.2
Developing countries	122	8.1	8.1
Centrally planned countries	435	21.3	28.7
	1,514	100.0	100.0

Trade in industrial products

A dominant trend in world trade during the postwar period is the growing importance of industrial products. It is above all the trade in high-technology products from the chemical and engineering industries that has expanded rapidly, both before and after the recession of 1974-5. This applies to practically all countries. The exchange of industrial goods forms the expanding sector of East-West trade — and the sector which encourages hopes of continued growth (8).

The important sectors of trade in industrial goods are nevertheless the internal trade within OECD and the trade between developing and industrialized countries. It is these trade flows that we shall take a closer look at here.

The internal trade of the OECD countries

The internal trade of the industrial countries in manufactured products is the important, dynamic component in world trade during the postwar period. In 1950 this trade constituted around 25 per cent of total world trade; in 1963 it had increased to about 30 per cent and in 1973, the year before the oil price-rises, to 38 per cent. The industrialized countries account for 82 per cent of world exports of manufactured products, and of that almost 70 per cent is their trade with one another.

It may seem paradoxical that the trade in industrial products to a large extent is sustained by the industrial countries' trade with each other. Should not industrialization make countries more self-sufficient with regard to manufactured products? An extensive discussion of this did actually take place during the early postwar period (9). Fairly soon, however, reality made the theoretical speculations irrelevant.

Yet there is still another paradox to explain. Not only is the industrial trade of the OECD countries with each other the fastest expanding sector of world trade. Within this internal trade the exchange of the same kind of products — the intra-industry trade — constitutes a growing proportion.

8. In Appendix 1, diagrams a-e, there is a summary of the geographical change in the pattern of trade during the postwar period.
9. See Maizels, pp. 4-5.

The economists Grubel and Lloyd have made a careful study of this intra-industry trade in the case of the ten leading industrial countries (10). For this group the share of intra-industry trade rises from 36 per cent in 1959 to 42 per cent in 1964 and 48 per cent in 1967. During the period investigated the intra-industry trade accounts for as much as 80 per cent of the growth in the total trade for the ten countries (11).

Great Britain has the highest as well as the most rapidly increasing intra-industry trade — now almost 70 per cent. Other countries with over 55 per cent are France, Belgium-Luxembourg, and the Netherlands. The United States, Canada, West Germany, and Italy fall in the range 42-49 per cent. The intra-industry trade is increasing faster than the average for the total trade in all of these countries. The intra-industry trade of Japan is relatively small — about 20 per cent — and the share increased very slightly during 1959-64 and not at all during 1964-69. Australia has the lowest share (12).

Among the commodity groups the most rapid increase is manufactured products. Trade in industrial goods therefore does not primarily mean that cars are exchanged for steel and chemical products for consumer durables. To an increasing extent the imports of cars and steel are paid for with exports of steel and cars.

The most important explanation lies partly in a highly advanced specialization in production, partly in a large increase of trade in components and semi-manufacturers in step with the organization of production processes on a global level (13). The exchange of steel and cars for steel and cars in actual fact represents an exchange of different steel grades or steel products for others, and of American luxury cars for European small cars.

10. Grubel & Lloyd. The ten countries included in the study are: Great Britain, France, Belgium-Luxembourg, the Netherlands, the United States, Canada, West Germany, Italy, Japan, and Australia. Unless anything to the contrary is stated the figures given in the text relate to comparisons of exports and imports at the so-called three-digit level in the commodity classification for international trade. Thus commodity groups of type SITC 611 Leather and SITC 641 Paper and Board are compared with each other.
11. Ibid., pp. 41-42.
12. Ibid., p. 38.
13. See below, section IV.4.

Only by concentrating on a narrow range can enterprises achieve sufficiently long production runs. Swedish manufacturers of bathtubs import the steel profiles from Japan because Swedish industry cannot afford to retool its machines merely for this particular product. Volvo does not just sell a car in the upper middle price range but tries consistently to promote certain features such as safety, reliability, and durability. Enterprises attempt by all available means, actual changes in production or advertising campaigns, to monopolize secure niches in the market — and these niches are constantly shrinking. The specialization of production has progressed further than the statistics that provide the basic data for trade reports.

Another important explanation of the increase in intra-industry trade is that parts, components and semi-manufactures are often registered within the same SITC class as the finished product. Thus when American companies dispatch inputs in order to have clothing, gloves, and baseballs made in the West Indies for re-export to the United States, that is intra-industry trade.

The same result is obtained when parts of Swiss watches are precision-drilled in Mauretania, when ammunition for the US Army is assembled in Mexico, and when Chinese in Singapore manufacture 'German' cameras. The transnational corporations have — at least since the end of the sixties — quickly exploited the opportunities for reducing costs by farming out labour-intensive stages of the production process to countries with low wages and an acceptable labour productivity.

These two main explanations in conjunction can also help to explain the low growth of productivity in the United States. American enterprises have such a large domestic market that they can already there exploit the advantages of large-scale operation provided by modern technology. Further specialization would only add marginally to this. For European enterprises, however, the opportunity for advanced specialization offered by international free trade produces large marginal advantages. It is likely, however, that development has now gone so far that further gains in productivity will become smaller and smaller. The newly industrialized countries, on the other hand, have great and simple chances of gains in productivity in a liberalized world economy.

The developing countries as a market

The developing countries' need to purchase industrial products, both for consumption and investments, is extensive. They often have ambitious industrialization programmes but a still limited productive capacity of their own. Industrial imports must therefore be paid for by exports of primary commodities. The purchasing power in a country can of course be increased by commercial loans and aid. In the main, however, it is the export surplus of primary commodities that determines the possible size of the imports of manufactured products. (See table A in Appendix 1.)

Thus stagnating revenues from the exports of primary commodities caused the developing countries' imports of industrial commodities from the OECD countries to increase very slowly during the 1950s. The prices of primary commodities fell drastically and a rapid increase in aid could only marginally improve the situation. During the sixties the situation was somewhat alleviated due to the stabilization of the terms of trade between primary commodities and manufactured products. The developing countries as a group were still heavily dependent on primary commodities, however, and the slow rise in the volume of these commodities retarded developing countries' capacity to purchase manufactured products from the OECD countries. Throughout the fifties and sixties the importance of the developing countries as a market for manufactured exports from OECD countries diminished. In the early 1950s the OECD countries sold almost a third of their exports of industrial commodities in the Third World. At the end of the 1960s the share was only a fifth.

This trend was radically interrupted during the 1970s. The main reason was the rise in oil prices. At one blow the purchasing power of the OPEC states was multiplied several times over. The importance of these countries as a market for exports from the OECD countries increased from 4–5 per cent in 1972 to about 11 per cent.

Oil-importing developing countries were severely affected by the higher oil prices. Nevertheless they maintained or extended their role as consumers of exports from the OECD countries. This development, which was largely financed by commercial loans, was sustained by 10-20 newly industrializing countries (14) and a few other mineral-rich developing countries. Despite the recession these countries were struggling to carry through their development plans. Their only chance of achieving them was to make use of export credits and to raise loans in the international capital market. This development was reflected in the large increase of deficits on the balance of current account of the non oil-exporting developing countries, demonstrated in table IV.3.

Table IV.3   Balance of current account of different groups of countries 1970-8 (billions of dollars, current prices)

	1970	1973	1974	1975	1976	1977	1978
OECD countries	4.0	3.0	-32.8	- 6.3	-24.5	-32.0	- 0.8
Centrally planned countries	-1.5	-5.5	- 9.8	-18.0	-13.3	-11.3	- 9.5
OPEC states	2.0	9.0	61.3	28.8	29.3	34.0	11.0
Non oil-exporting developing countries	-6.8	-8.0	-24.0	-39.5	-26.5	-26.5	-34.0

Source: Herin, p. 56.

A similar development was taking place in the South European countries and in the Eastern bloc states. Countries like Greece, Yugoslavia, Spain, and Turkey raised considerable loans during the 1970s in order to maintain imports. A large proportion of the OECD countries' deficit on current account in table IV.3 was accounted for by the South European members. The East European states allowed themselves during the seventies to

14. These countries are introduced in the next section. They are moderately wealthy developing countries that have progressed a fair distance with their industrialization and are succeeding well as exporters of manufactured products.

accumulate heavy debts to the West in order to be able to carry out their ambitious investment programmes.

The consequence of the development outlined here is that the old industrial countries have become increasingly dependent on external markets. This is particularly evident in the case of advanced capital goods. The volume of investment diminished greatly in the OECD countries during the second half of the seventies at the same time as developing countries and Eastern bloc states carried out their credit-financed investment programmes. In the case of a number of typical capital goods such as 'machinery for specialized industries' and 'other machinery and transport equipment' over 50 per cent of the total exports now go to countries outside the OECD (15).

The newly industrializing countries

The old industrial countries still play a dominant role in the world economy but their importance is declining. GDP and industrial output rise more slowly in the wealthy market economies than in Eastern Europe and many developing countries.

This is a natural as well as inevitable development. In an internationalized world economy with efficient communications, an extensive diffusion of knowledge and a globalized production process, the dynamics of industrialism must be self-propagating. New countries and regions appear as centres of growth and gradually catch up with the former pioneer countries. Great Britain was the first, and it took almost a century before its position was seriously threatened. The United States strengthened its leading position through two economically successful world wars. But it took only 20-25 years for the other OECD countries to catch up with the American technological lead.

The preconditions for industrial production have radically improved during the postwar period in a number of countries outside North America, Western Europe, and Japan. The infrastructure has been extended and investments in education have multiplied several times over in Asia, Africa, and Latin America. At the same time the wage level is only a fraction of the average

15.GATT: *International Trade 1977/78*, table K.

in the OECD region. The mobility of enterprises and their ability to organize production are continually improved. In several branches of industry the dominant technology is generally known and accessible to those with sufficient knowledge to make use of it. With regard to almost all the preconditions for industrial production — the health and education of the labour force, technical competence, research, infrastructure, freight costs, managerial expertise, and organizational ability — a number of developing countries will continue to improve markedly their *relative* position vis-à-vis the old industrialized countries. In addition, these newly industrializing countries will have a considerably better demographic structure — an increasing proportion of the population at a productive age — while the proportion of elderly grows in the old industrial countries (16).

It is thus a natural process when the growth poles of capitalism move away from the areas where the technological gains and the long production runs are already fully exploited. Obviously, the move need not be from one country to another. Within the United States, enterprises and investment capital today move in a rapid stream from the industrialized states in the north to lower wages and weaker trade unions in the 'sun belt' of the south (17). In France the old coal and steel areas stagnate while the industries of the future flourish in the Mediterranean area (18).

The fastest industrial expansion is occurring today in the 10-20 new industrial countries in the Third World. Some states are self-evident members of this group. South Korea and Taiwan have during the last fifteen years or more achieved an unusually rapid increase in production and export of manufactured products. Even in an absolute sense they play a certain role in the world market. The rate of expansion of Brazil and Mexico is not quite as impressive and is less stable, but they possess a considerable proportion of the combined industry of the Third World. The two city-states of Hong Kong and Singapore are among the fastest expanding countries in the world, even though their absolute importance is small. Other obvious candidates are the

16. The internationalization of the production process is extensively dealt with by Staffan Laestadius (1980).
17. Åkerman: *Georgia*.
18. *The Mediterranean Growth and Investment Area.*

newly industrializing countries in Southern Europe — Portugal, Spain, Yugoslavia, Greece, and Turkey. Romania should possibly also be included.

Among the less self-evident newly industrializing countries are Malaysia, Thailand, the Philippines, Indonesia, India, and Colombia, as well as several smaller states in Central America and the Caribbean region. It is impossible to draw a clear border-line, and this underscores one important fact. The newly industrializing countries are not a unique group — they have simply progressed furthest in a development that is general if not yet universal in the Third World. The industrial sector is slowly but surely becoming more important for the output, employment, and exports of almost all developing countries. Table IV.4 shows that the importance of industrial products is increasing very rapidly. If one excludes oil, which is possessed by only a few countries, industrial products even today account for almost half of the export value of the developing countries.

Table IV.4   Industrial products (SITC 5-8) as a proportion of total exports excluding fuels 1960-76 (percentage share)

	1960	1965	1970	1972	1974	1975	1976
Whole world	61.1	65.4	71.4	73.0	72.8	74.0	74.4
Industrialized countries	70.3	72.7	78.1	78.6	78.5	79.2	79.7
Centrally planned countries	67.2	71.2	68.4	71.5	68.5	70.3	66.7
Developing countries	19.5	25.4	35.1	38.3	42.4	42.6	45.1

Source: UNIDO (1979), p. 141.

The interesting question now is what the rapid expansion in the newly industrialising countries will mean for the OECD countries and for the chances of creating a working international trade order.

The newly industrializing countries are likely to have a strong interest in preserving a stable order with free trade, convertible currencies, and free capital movements — if possible with continued opportunities for free-riding. The question is whether the OECD countries will succeed in integrating the newly industrializing countries into that order.

The relationship between new and old industrial countries

The central question concerns employment in the OECD countries — and this has been the focus in a number of studies on the relations between new and old industrial countries (19). The methods employed in these studies are often very simple. Some of them amount to no more than rambling discussions of various alternatives. Others use input-output analysis to study what happens if imports and exports increase simultaneously by a certain amount. The net change in employment is then due to the fact that the industry that is knocked out by imports from developing countries is more or less labour-intensive than the expanding exporting industry. Another common method is to calculate the effect of various future alternatives estimated on the basis of the development of trade during the last 5-10 years. In that way an interval for likely changes in the future is 'bracketed' in. Several studies deal only with the effects of increased imports from developing countries, often in only some of the threatened industries. Indirect effects are often ignored.

Despite the variation in methodology the conclusions of the studies are remarkably unanimous:

19.The account given in this section is based chiefly on the following studies of the relations between old and new industrial countries: Berthelot & Tardy (France); Commissariat Général du Plan (France); Noelke (EEC countries); *European Economic Community and Changes in the International Division of Labour* (report by a group of experts, with studies of individual EEC countries); Giersch (1976); UNIDO: *The Impact of Trade with Developing Countries on Employment in Developed Countries* (review of a large number of studies); Kierzkowski (Sweden); and *The Newly Industrializing Countries and the Adjustment Problem* (Great Britain). This list naturally presents no claim to completeness but, bearing in mind the unanimity in respect of conclusions, it is adequate for the purpose of this discussion. Some empirical material on the newly industrializing countries is found in Anell: *De nya industrilanderna.*

— according to all of the studies the total effect of continued balanced trade with developing countries will be negative but very small (20). Several studies compare the effects of continued rationalization of production and of imports from developing countries. Many times more jobs are lost because of improved production technology (21).

— nearly all the studies maintain that the effects in future will be more negative than at present though still small and manageable.

— the industries primarily affected by imports from developing countries are clothing, footwear, leather, and textiles. Also parts of the labour-intensive engineering and instrument industry move out to low-wage countries. This applies, for example, to the manufacturing of optical and precision instruments, electro-engineering, and precision mechanics. Industries that manufacture simple consumer goods are mentioned in several of the studies as being among those that will experience a net decrease in employment.

— several of the studies show that the negative effects will be strongest for regions that are already weak and for groups of people that are lacking in resources. German and French studies point out that the imports from developing countries exacerbate the regional problems. Among the groups that are affected some of the studies mention women and, in West Germany, migrant workers. Authors of studies on the effects on the British economy, on the contrary, find no evidence of negative regional or distributive effects.

All the authors of these studies take care to emphasize that the methods employed are so rough and ready that the results can only be regarded as preliminary. On the other hand, we observe that the results tend to support each other. We can be fairly certain that the conclusions presented are valid. The question is whether the studies relate to the real problem.

As several of the studies point out, it is the net effect of both imports from and exports to the developing countries that deter-

---

20. It could be claimed that Vincent Cable (in *The European Economic Community and Changes in the International Division of Labour*) goes a step further when he maintains that he can find hardly any net effect at all.
21. Wolter's study (in Giersch, 1976) is particularly illuminating in this respect.

mines whether total employment in a country will increase or diminish. But the governments in the OECD countries cannot reduce the problem to one applying only to *net* changes in employment. They must look at the gross effect. The problem concerns all who become unemployed because of increased imports. The new jobs in industries which export defence material, heavy lorries, and automatic telephone exchanges to developing countries may not suit those who become unemployed in the ready-made clothing, footwear, and leather industries. In several studies it is also evident that the jobs lost and those gained are not located in the same region.

It is only in the British study that the observation is made that the net problem in itself may be small — but it is superimposed on a problem that is already sizeable: the currently existing unemployment in the OECD countries (22). None of the studies that I have consulted makes any systematic attempt to consider the effects of competition from developing countries in third countries. The British study is again the only one that even refers to this question (23). It is also hard to see how one can differentiate between jobs that are lost because of low-wage competition and those which disappear as a result of technological rationalization of production. Measures to make production more efficient may in fact be due to foreign competition.

The most serious criticism of the above-mentioned studies, however, is that they do not deal with the future net balance in the trade between old and new industrial countries. The OECD countries have a large surplus of trade in manufactured products with third countries. From 1963 to 1970 this surplus increased at current prices from $ 19 billion to $ 34 billion. The increase continued during the first years of the seventies but then only in step with inflation. During the recession of 1973-5 the OECD countries' surplus increased from $ 53 billion to $ 117 billion, which at fixed prices represented an increase of about 50 per cent. In 1976 there was a minor decline, followed by a small rise in 1977.

The most interesting point here is the large increase in the OECD countries' export of manufactured products to third

22.*The Newly Industrializing* . . ., p. viii.
23.Op. cit., p. iv.

countries during the crisis of 1974-5. What happened then was that demand fell drastically in the old industrial countries. The crisis was, as I have shown earlier, confined to the OECD region. Simultaneously, the OPEC states used a large proportion of their increased oil revenue to step up imports of industrial products, especially capital equipment. The Eastern bloc states and many developing countries continued to increase their imports of manufactured products in 1974-5 and they financed this by borrowing money in the international capital markets.

In this process newly industrializing countries played a central and an interesting role. For several years GDP and exports had been increasing very rapidly in these countries. Industrialization had taken root, the comparative advantages for industrial production were gradually being reinforced, and the forecasts for continued increases in the export of manufactured products were very optimistic. In that situation there was no reason to abandon ambitious investment plans because of what was assumed to be a temporary crisis in the OECD countries.

The newly industrializing countries borrowed the money they needed to continue buying the desired capital equipment. The outcome was naturally one of growing deficits in the balance of trade and of current account. A group of twenty countries, of which the majority belong to the category of newly industrializing countries, financed enormous deficits in the balance of trade in connection with the crisis during the 1970s. An import surplus of $ 12-20 billion in the early 1970s grew to $ 45-60 billion in 1974-5 (24). The imports that were not paid for with current incomes from exports were for the most part financed by purely commercial loans. Various studies indicate that this credit-financed demand from developing countries in general and from newly industrializing countries in particular must have saved 2-3 million jobs in the OECD countries (25).

24. Anell & Nygren, pp. 96-8. The twenty countries are Brazil, Mexico, Peru, Panama, Morocco, Egypt, Sudan, Yemen, the Philippines, Singapore, Thailand, South Korea, Pakistan, India, Israel, and five south European countries: Greece, Yugoslavia, Spain, Turkey, and Gibraltar.

25. Noelke (1978) suggests that the developing countries saved about 2 million jobs, page v. See also Blackhurst et al.: *Adjustment*, pp. 13-4. In France 100,000 jobs were saved during 1970-6 thanks to the trade with the Third World, according to Berthelot & Tardy, p. 9. With regard to commercial borrowing to finance the deficits, see Noelke (1979), p. 101.

The question now is how the net balance of trade between new and old industrial countries will evolve in future. It is rather pointless to prove that the employment effects will be small if exports to and imports from newly industrializing countries increase by the same amount. The important thing is to consider whether such a balanced process is realistic.

According to the rules of the game the newly industrializing countries will, of course, at some time in the future create an export surplus in order to repay the money that has been borrowed. If so, that will happen through the pursuit by the governments of those countries of an economic policy that restrains demand and imports at the same time as exports are stimulated. For the OECD countries that would then mean that an important export market stagnates at the same time as low-wage competition is intensified. And the changes involved are not marginal. The annual deficits in the balance of trade that were financed with credits in the mid-1970s by the twenty countries concerned represented about 5 per cent of world exports.

There are several signs that some of the newly industrializing countries have already begun moving towards a balance or net surplus on foreign trade. The OECD countries' surplus on trade in industrial commodities with the newly industrializing countries declined fairly drastically in 1974-5 (26). The OECD countries' surplus also appears to have stagnated in their trade with all non oil-exporting developing countries. As shown in table IV.5 the industrialized countries' surplus on their trade in industrial goods with non oil-exporting developing countries increased very strongly from 1972 to 1975 but subsequently stagnated at a level of $ 42-3 billion at current prices.

The OECD countries show a growing deficit in their net trade in an increasing number of commodity groups. So far it is still mainly a case of light standardized consumer goods, but the exports of the newly industrializing countries are increasing most

26. These calculations apply to a group of newly industrializing countries that includes Brazil, Greece, Hong Kong, South Korea, Mexico, Portugal, Singapore, Spain, Taiwan, and Yugoslavia. See also the change in the balance of payments for, e.g., Colombia, South Korea, Malaysia, Taiwan, Argentina, Hong Kong, and India in *World Development Report 1979*, table 13.

rapidly with regard to capital- and R & D-intensive products (27).

Table IV.5   Trade in industrial products between developing and industrial countries 1953-77 ($ billion at current prices)

	1953	1963	1972	1975	1977
Exports from developing to industrialized countries	(0.6)	3.08	12.09	22.85	36.20
Imports to developing from industrialized countries	(13.5)	16.97	40.76	105.35	135.65
Difference	(12.9)	13.89	28.67	85.20	99.45
Exports from OPEC states to industrialized countries	—	—	0.28	0.75	1.10
Imports to OPEC states from industrialized countries	—	—	9.69	40.25	57.90
Difference			9.41	39.50	56.80
Exports from other developing countries to industrialized countries	—	—	11.70	21.90	35.10
Imports to other developing countries from industrialized countries	—	—	30.73	64.85	77.75
Difference			19.03	42.95	42.65

Source: Various annual volumes of GATT *International Trade*, and UNCTAD: *Handbook 1976* and *Supplement 1977*.

27. Regarding net trade in various products see Blackhurst et al.: *Adjustment*, p. 33; Noelke (1978), pp. 186-9, and Noelke (1979), p. 64, for EEC trade with the Third World; Ensor, pp. 29-30, for US trade with the Third World; and Boston Consulting Group, Appendix 9, pp. 8-9, for the trade of certain smaller countries with developing countries. The rapid expansion with regard to more sophisticated products is demonstrated in Chenery & Keesing, pp. 32-3, and UNIDO (1979), p. 154.

If several of the newly industrializing countries in the near future choose or, due to difficulties in obtaining credits, are forced to pursue a restrictive economic policy at home combined with aggressive competition in the export markets, this will have immediate consequences. From having contributed to the stability of the world economy by saving 2-3 million jobs during the deep recession, the newly industrializing countries would in that case come to play a destabilizing role.

The problem is manageable even if it demands a generosity and co-ordination that have so far not been typical of economic foreign policy in the OECD countries (28). It is not a question of a zero sum game. The first priority is to avoid forcing the newly industrializing countries to phase out prematurely their deficits in the balance of trade. In the long term it should be possible to complete that process in step with the increase in the gross volume of trade and production.

We can therefore sum up by stating that a continuing balanced trade with the newly industrializing countries involves problems that are in themselves not intractable. They are, however, superimposed on problems that are already sizeable. We cannot expect the newly industrializing countries and developing countries to 'solve' the employment problems of the OECD countries in the future in the same way as they did during the crisis of 1974-5 (29). It is likely that the trade with newly industrializing countries during the 1980s will have an adverse effect on employment in the OECD region. The import surpluses will be reduced. Problems of structural adjustment will be exacerbated due to the fact that it will become a matter of both traditional adaptation within a branch of industry and horizontal structural adjustment between branches. Even if these problems are in themselves small, they may affect the possibilities for the OECD governments to maintain a free trade order. One way of putting it is whether North America and Western Europe can manage 'another Japan' during the 1980s. One should then remember, however,

28. It is indeed quite possible that it will not be feasible to co-ordinate the actions of the OECD countries. If so, the Third World might well, as Ben Evers predicts, become the main arena for a commercial confrontation between the central blocs — EEC, Japan, and the United States (*The European Economic Community*, p. 15).
29. Anell & Nygren, pp. 96-7.

that it will be a matter of producing industrial commodities for six billion people in the year 2000 and for nine billion twenty-five years later (30). Theoretically there is thus considerable scope for co-operation.

The transnational corporations — organization and adaptation

Two motives have so far dominated the foreign establishment of the transnational corporations: an endeavour to control the supply of primary commodities, and a need to maintain and expand market positions. The latter motive is reinforced by the fact that the developing countries have often introduced almost prohibitive tariffs on imports of manufactured productions, and by the establishment of the Common Market in Europe in 1958. The American corporations in particular have invested in the expanding EEC market.

During the 1960s a third important motive began to emerge — the chance of exploiting low wages in the developing countries. This linked up with several changes in the world economy. Prevailing stability made developing countries appear to be less and less risky. Freight costs diminished and air freight became economically feasible. Data- and satellite-based information systems were developed. Business management was internationalized. All of this made it possible to organize production on a global scale. By breaking down production into separate processes, the most labour-intensive phases could be farmed out. This development was also promoted by the tariff legislation in some of the OECD countries (31).

Probably, however, the low-wage motive is still weaker than the other two main motives. One investigation shows that only a tenth of the foreign investments can be characterized as low-wage investments (32). It seems evident, however, that low wages combined with high labour productivity exert an increasingly

30.*Interfutures*, pp. 11-15.
31.See, among others, Salera, p. 5, on the internationalization of business management, and Schiller, p. 8, on an emerging cosmopolitan business culture. The sub-division and internationalization of the production process is dealt with by Laestadius (1979 and 1980).
32.*The European Economic Community*, p. 16.

powerful attraction (33). The EEC study indicates that roughly
a third of the foreign investments in Asia have been motivated
by an endeavour to exploit low wages.

Towards a new organization

The traditional image of the transnational corporation is still one
of a parent company with large holdings in a number of subsidiary companies. This image remains by and large correct. The
majority of the American and Western European transnational
corporations are still organized around a number of owned and
controlled production enterprises in various parts of the world.
Many of the large international corporations reveal a strong
preference for wholly owned subsidiary companies.

But a new kind of transnational organizations is emerging.
They base their position on control of markets and trademarks
and concentrate on organizing the production process without
necessarily owning the participating enterprises. It may not even
be desirable to tie up capital in fixed plants. The pioneers in this
area were the large Japanese corporations which in several
respects operate in the form of gigantic trading houses (34). The
idea is now rapidly being copied by large department stores,
retail chain stores, and wholesale companies in Europe and the
United States. A growing number of transnational corporations
are thus organized from the consumption side in relatively loose-
knit international systems with varying memberships (35). The
leading enterprise is chiefly responsible for marketing, product
design, planning, and organization; perhaps also for financing,
but with a limited involvement of its own capital.

This 'Japanese model' is obviously uniquely adapted to a world
economy in which instability is increasing and nationalism in the
developing countries is growing. To a large extent these new

33. Lall & Streeten, p. 29.
34. This is not a revolutionizing concept, however. Unilever, which owns over 100,000
    trademarks, in several ways resembles a trading house (UNCTAD: *Transnational
    Corporations*, p. 17), as do several of the old colonial trading firms (see for instance
    Sveriges samarbete med u-länderna, SOU 1977:13, p. 83). Jurg Niehaus describes
    the Swiss-based transnational corporation Brown, Boveri & Cie virtually as an
    international system (Agmon & Kindleberger, p. 24).
35. UNCTAD: *Transnational Corporations*, p. 11.

enterprises evade the sensitive question of proprietary control of the subsidiary companies in the developing countries. There are quite simply no production installations to nationalize. The trading-house enterprises are also able to adapt themselves quickly to new market conditions. It is easy to expand promising lines of production through collaboration with new enterprises. There are few heavy investments to tie the enterprises to stagnating branches. The liquidation of less profitable products can be achieved by severing links with various independent enterprises.

Intrafirm trade

The rapid expansion of the transnational corporations — especially during the 1960s — and their strong position in world trade have some interesting consequences for the world economy. One important effect is that a growing and now very large part of world trade takes place within one and the same enterprise (intrafirm trade) or between associated enterprises in which the parent company has a minority holding (related party trade). C. A. Michalet calculated that around 45 per cent of total world trade consists of intrafirm trade (36). A leading authority in this field, the Canadian economist Gerry Helleiner, calculates that around one-fifth of the United States' exports in 1970 went to majority-owned subsidiary companies, while as much as 66 per cent were 'associated with US-based transnational enterprises'. In the case of imports the corresponding proportions were 16 and 46 per cent (37). In the case of American exports of industrial products the UNCTAD secretariat estimates that roughly half went to majority-owned subsidiary companies overseas (38).

36. Michalet, quoted in *European Economic Community*, p. 1. The definitions of intrafirm trade vary, thus causing the mathematical calculations to differ as well. Michalet's calculation is the highest that I have come across. The UNCTAD secretariat expresses itself more cautiously and estimates that over 30 per cent of total world trade is intrafirm (UNCTAD: *Transnational Corporations*, p. 1). Transnational corporations and their growing internal trade are fairly extensively dealt with by Staffan Laestadius (1980). See also Radice, pp. 100 et seq.
37. Helleiner: *Intrafirm trade*, p. 8.
38. UNCTAD: *Transnational Corporations*, p. 1. See also Barnet & Müller, who are convinced 'that at least 50 per cent of all US exports are by-passing the market', i.e. they occur between enterprises controlled by the same groups of owners (pp. 266-7).

It seems evident that both the intrafirm trade and the related-party trade in industrial products are increasing faster than total world trade. What may appear surprising is that it is above all within the OECD group that this trade is growing. This could be due to the fact that a proportion of the imports from developing countries on the 'Japanese model' do not qualify as related-party trade (39). Another interesting trend is that imports of primary commodities from the developing countries are to a decreasing extent of an intrafirm nature. Helleiner believes that 'the break-up of the old order in world minerals markets . . . is now well under way' (40).

Transnational corporations nevertheless still play a dominant role in the trade in all primary commodities except possibly jute, hides, and skins (41). Normally over half of the world's production, processing, and sales are controlled by less than ten enterprises. The position of the Seven Sisters in the oil market is still strong. Three enterprises market and distribute 70 per cent of the world production of bananas (42). In the case of bauxite and aluminium six enterprises are responsible for 60 and 70 per cent respectively of the world's production capacity (43).

Besides the intrafirm trade and related-party trade, there is a growing trade on the basis of subcontracting. This normally takes the form of an importing enterprise being responsible for product design, supplying patented technology and loans for investments, while the producing enterprises deliver the agreed quantity. This is 'intrafirm' trade on the Japanese trading-house model. Morton and Tulloch estimate that as much as 50-80 per cent of exports of manufactured products from Asian developing countries may be subcontracted (44).

It may also be worth mentioning another tendency that contributes towards a situation in which a constantly decreasing proportion of world trade consists of normal market transactions

39. If the leading enterprise does not have a minority holding or owns less than 5 per cent of the share capital in the enterprises with which it collaborates, the trade between the parties falls outside current definitions of related-party trade.
40. Helleiner: *Structural Aspects*, p. 12.
41. UNCTAD: *Transnational Corporations*, p. 2.
42. Payer, p. 132.
43. A careful examination of the role of transnational enterprises in the international raw material markets is found in Hollander & Tegen.
44. Morton & Tulloch, p. 212.

between buyers and sellers who are independent of each other. Not only is an increasing share of the international exchange of goods and services taking place within one and the same enterprise or group of owners, but the trade organized or influenced by governments is also growing in importance. Large arms deals, civil engineering projects, and orders for the public sector are now normally accompanied by government participation in the negotiations (45). The market forces are at present as much politico-administrative as economic. We should remember this when we later worry about whether the international free trade order may change (46).

Instability and adjustment

An important effect of the tendencies outlined above is that changes now occur very rapidly. Transnational corporations, like other enterprises, desire stability, yet they are nevertheless likely to be able to adjust to altered circumstances faster and more efficiently than other international agents (47).

The transnational trading houses in particular are very flexible. An efficient local production unit in a developing country is never far away from an established international distribution network. A leading enterprise that initiates efficient production in a developing country soon creates a bandwagon effect. Within the electronics industry a serious search for low-wage countries began in 1967 (48). Fairchilds started producing electronic components in Singapore at the end of the 1960s. Within 3-4 years that country became a leading producer of semiconductors in Asia, second only to Japan (49). But during the latter half of the 1970s some of the electronics enterprises already began to move production 'back home' to California due to changes of production techniques. Hong Kong, South Korea, and Japan in a very short space of time captured three-quarters of the British

45. A current review of this 'state trade' is available in Kostecki. See also Hudson, pp. 230-1, and Calleo, p. 72.
46. Diaz-Alejandro.
47. Helleiner, pp. 28-29.
48. Keesing, p. 54.
49. Fong & Lim, p. 12.
50. *The Newly Industrializing Countries*, p. 39. See also Minian, pp. 134 ff.

market for stainless cutlery. Singapore's share of Great Britain's imports of hygienic and pharmaceutical rubber goods increased from 1970 to 1976 from 0.5 to 36 per cent (51).

Another important effect of the way that the transnational corporations organize the world economy is that mobility increases. The alternative opportunities for locating production and combining chains of production are multiplying.

The dependence of enterprises on physical location factors is usually slight. In several of the expanding industries, fixed investments are relatively small. Formerly, enterprises may have been tied to regions with mineral resources, a power supply, skilled labour, and proximity to markets. We now have a development on several levels that makes enterprises more and more footloose. The basic industries, which are tied to heavy fixed investments and raw material resources, are declining in importance both in relation to their share of value added and to employment. Enterprises are becoming increasingly adept at freeing themselves from dependence on skilled labour. The production processes can be broken down into simple phases that can be carried out by unskilled labour.

There are several signs indicating greater caution with regard to traditional overseas investments during the 1970s, particularly since the oil crisis and the deep recession during 1973-5. Investments in extractive industries in developing countries have declined greatly in recent years. In other areas, too, firms seem to hesitate to make binding new investments (52). New investments are mainly in improved machinery, more rarely for real expansion of production capacity. In general, enterprises appear to shorten their planning periods and to attach greater importance to the need for quick adaptability. The attempts to organize more loosely-knit transnational enterprises are probably partly an adaptation to the increasing instability in the world economy — and to the growing nationalism in the Third World.

The present situation may be described roughly as follows. The preconditions for industrial production continue to improve in the newly industrializing countries as compared with the situation in the OECD countries. At the same time, firms are

51. *The Newly Industrializing Countries*, p. v.
52. Herin, pp. 48-50; Ensor, pp. 118-9; *Interfutures*, pp. 112-33; Glyn & Sutcliffe, p. 58

becoming increasingly hesitant in exploiting these potential opportunities for improving production efficiency (53). We get a growing gap between the actual international division of labour and the one desired by the enterprises and believers in the benefits of free trade. The reason for this situation is primarily, as Blackhurst et al. have put it, that 'uncertainty is a highly effective non-tariff barrier to international trade, in particular because it discourages long-term investments whose profitability depends on secure access to foreign markets or on assured supplies of low-cost imported inputs' (54).

53. It may be worth mentioning that certain forms of instability can boost internationalization, on the principle that eggs should be placed in more than one basket. Increased foreign exchange risks, for example, may be a reason for having production in several currency areas (Agmon & Kindleberger, p. 13).

54. Blackhurst et al.: *Trade Liberalization*, p. 8. It should be added here that it is only in certain spheres that the transnational enterprises desire stability and order. Many industrial groups are fairly satisfied with the present profitable anarchy in respect of the law of the sea (*From Marshall Plan*, p. 192), and with regard to outer space the United States is also doubtful about increased order (Schiller, p. 65).

V. THE NATION STATE AND THE INTERNATIONAL ORDER

> Progress would be wonderful — if only it would stop.
>
> *Robert Musil*

> Liberty means responsibility. That is why most men dread it.
>
> *G.B. Shaw*

Most theories about international relations in both political science and in economics are based on the idea that national states are rational entities capable of establishing well-defined goals. This, like all scientific models, is a deliberate simplification. The political scientists assume that governments can reconcile conflicting interests in forming national goals and the economists assume that the market mechanism achieves an effective allocation of productive resources.

Obviously, the role that the national state plays in these models is open to discussion. But the question is whether this perspective is tenable. Is it possible to analyse international conditions by assuming that the national entities have certain definite characteristics? At all events, my angle of approach is quite the opposite. I suggest that we can only have an international order which is nationally acceptable; the world order is a derivative of the internal conditions of nations making up the international community.

This statement should be clarified. The international system consists of national states with more or less democratically elected governments. There is no international régime which can — formally at least — impose its will on a sovereign state.

The leading industrialized countries in the OECD are all democracies. There is a strong consensus supporting this form of government which lends legitimacy to governments' exercise of power. Many, possibly a definite majority of the citizens, may be dissatisfied with a government's actions but extremely few question its right to take them. The government has the exclusive right to the legitimate exercise of power and is assumed to be solely responsible for the development of the country.

There are international agreements and conventions which have been given a certain degree of legitimacy by the fact that the legislative assembly has accepted them. There is also a certain amount of understanding of the fact that international crises can place the government in an emergency situation. Rationing and other restrictions such as those caused by the first oil crisis meet few objections. But in the main, the situation is nonetheless as Stanley Hoffman describes it:

> The international economy, manipulated by its members, operates as a constant but unpredictable system of double distribution — of incomes, jobs, status within nations, and wealth and power among nations. But the domestic victims of this redistribution do not acknowledge the legitimacy of a haphazard or shifty mechanism that is external to the nation and competes or conflicts with the internal redistribution schemes that have been legitimately, authoritatively, or imperatively set up within the confines of the nation (1).

This forces a government — once again in Hoffman's words — 'to look at the issues created by interdependence through the lenses shaped by their domestic experience' (2). There are many examples of stands taken in foreign affairs which are the outcome of domestic problems. France's strong support of the European Community is largely a part of its agricultural policy. The Italian Christian Democrats saw NATO and the EEC as allies in the struggle against the communists (3). The United States' plans for

1. Hoffman, p. 195 in *From Marshall Plan*.
2. Op. cit., p. 184.
3. See, for example, Ambassador Egidio Ortona's statement in *From Marshall Plan*, p. 203-4.

the postwar economic order were regarded as part of a necessary security policy. The IMF and the UN Security Council were, in the words of the US Secretary of Treasury, Henry Morgenthau, the two blades of a pair of scissors (4). In recent years, heads of governments in many countries have chased after feathers to put in their foreign-policy caps in order to improve their popularity prior to elections.

A government finds itself playing the role of broker. It must distribute available resources — money, food, land, power, jobs, and prestige — between all the conflicting interests which can make themselves felt. The art is to mete out the portions according to the potential power of the different groups. This is the way to cement a national will (aggregated consensus). Governments now have to play this role of broker in a world economy which has become so interdependent that it undermines national autonomy, i.e. the real power to manage the domestic economy. What is happening is, according to Assar Lindbeck, that 'at the same time that national governments have become more anxious to control the domestic economies — in terms of stabilization, allocation, and distribution policies — the autonomy of national economic policy has fallen' (5).

But the internationalization process entails — or has at any rate entailed so far — advantages for the participating OECD economies. The most important point is that the available material resources are greater, thanks to extensive division of labour. Thus, internationalization means that in exchange for a more restricted national autonomy (which makes the role of broker more difficult) governments get more resources to distribute (which makes the role of broker easier). This balance must remain clearly to the advantage (6) of the major governments to ensure the proper functioning of the order.

An international order may perhaps persist for quite a long time by virtue of an intrinsic inertia, the lack of options, and — above all — the difficulty of individual countries to 'opt out' on

---

4. Calleo, p. ix. See also Kreinin, p. 314, on United States support of European integration as an element in security policy.
5. Lindbeck in *From Marshall Plan*, p. 79.
6. I have shown in Section I.3 why it is not enough for the advantages to weigh only slightly more than the disadvantages.

their own. The existing order has over the past 20 to 25 years helped to mould the national orders into a cohesive organic entity with a close network of vital arteries and common nerve-centres. An amputation injures the whole organism but the amputated limb perishes. To go its own way is not regarded as a realistic alternative for the individual country.

Nevertheless, an order which does not deliver the goods must start to function more and more poorly. If governments do not get increasing real resources to distribute, they will not be able to cope with the broker function in fully democratic societies with strong interest groups. The crux in relations between the national state and the international order is the capability of governments to make long-term rational decisions.

These are the questions I shall discuss in the following section. My arguments are based on the following assumption: all OECD governments consider that international free trade is superior to all other known systems. There seems to be no doubt that this is a justifiable assumption in the light of the latest GATT negotiations — the Tokyo Round. We must keep in mind, however, some pronouncements from the European Commission, inspired by the French, about 'organized markets'. And there is an influential group of economists in the United Kingdom who definitely advocate increased protection for British industry.

My assumption implies that governments will strive to preserve and consolidate free trade. To do this, they must succeed in preventing too much 'free-riding' (7) and convince the strong domestic interest groups of the advantages of the prevailing order. The question is, then, the ability of governments to impose the structural adjustments that participation in a free-trade world order requires.

The role of the government

Democratically elected governments in OECD countries today have basically the same kind of broker role as the chosen representatives of the upper classes had at the end of the 19th and beginning of the 20th century. What has changed drastically,

---

7. This term is discussed in section I.3.

however, is the kind of society and cultural environment in which a national community of values has to be built and preserved. Most of the OECD countries have developed into pluralistic democracies with expert-manned interest groups during the 20th century. Scales of values are gradually becoming more egalitarian — the equality which previously only existed before the law is now being demanded in an increasing number of fields. At the same time the government-broker has to take decisions on a growing number of questions of increasing complexity. To put it bluntly, the late postwar period has seen increasingly weak governments trying to cope with more and increasingly complex problems — and this development will soon reach critical dimensions.

Diagram V.I is a schematic illustration of one important reason for the changed broker role of government. The development outlined there is representative primarily of north-west Europe but is also largely applicable to other OECD countries.

Figure 1 in the diagram is an attempt to illustrate the situation of government in the hierarchical society of the early 20th century. An upper class of capital owners, bourgeoisie, top-level officials, and large landowners had a monopoly of power and authority (8). Government and the bureaucracy were recruited from the upper classes. A 'national' consensus was achieved because all those who have power saw problems from the same upper-class angle. The only reason why the government and the upper-class circles are not entirely identical is that the politicians had some aspirations in the field of foreign policy and — not so often — as regards a pacifying social policy; aspirations of which the upper classes were explicitly sceptical. In any case, the dominating feature is the community of values (the area where the circles overlap).

There were conflicts within the upper classes between industrial and landowner interests, for instance on the question of tariff policy. But in all essentials, unity reigned. The central goal was to maintain the social order. Wages should be kept down so that companies could earn enough money to keep on investing.

8. Power is here defined as the actual means to allocate, control, and manipulate the resources of the community. Authority is vested in those whose power is accepted as legitimate by virtue of laws, custom, or public opinion.

Diagram V.1 The changed broker role of governments in European welfare economies 1900-80.

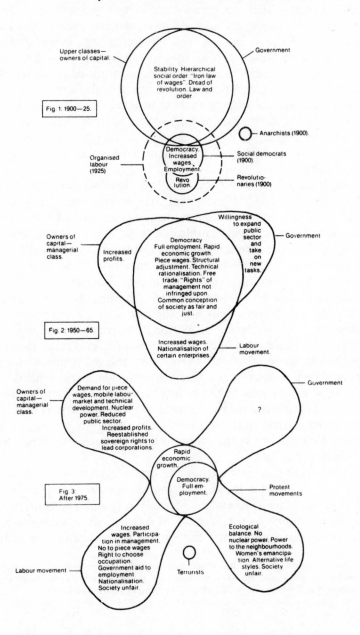

Fig. 1: 1900—25.

Upper classes—owners of capital.

Government

Stability. Hierarchical social order. "Iron law of wages". Dread of revolution. Law and order.

Anarchists (1900).

Social democrats (1900).

Democracy. Increased wages. Employment.

Revolution.

Revolutionaries (1900)

Organised labour (1925)

Fig. 2: 1950—65.

Owners of capital—managerial class.

Increased profits.

Democracy. Full employment. Rapid economic growth. Piece wages. Structural adjustment. Technical rationalisation. Free trade. "Rights" of management not infringed upon. Common conception of society as fair and just.

Willingness to expand public sector and take on new tasks.

Government

Increased wages. Nationalisation of certain enterprises.

Labour movement.

Fig. 3: After 1975.

Owners of capital—managerial class.

Demand for piece wages, mobile labour market and technical development. Nuclear power. Reduced public sector. Increased profits. Reestablished sovereign rights to lead corporations.

Government

?

Rapid economic growth.

Democracy. Full employment.

Protest movements

Increased wages. Participation in management. No to piece wages. Right to choose occupation. Government aid to employment. Nationalisation. Society unfair.

Labour movement

Terrorists

Ecological balance. No nuclear power. Power to the neighbourhoods. Women's emancipation. Alternative life styles. Society unfair.

A certain amount of public relief for the poor and elementary education could be tolerated, but any inclination to expect public relief as a right had to be combated. It was not only a matter of the upper classes defending their privileges — it was just as much a firm belief in a natural order.

But the overwhelming majority of citizens in these communities were small farmers, farm labourers, and industrial workers, who lived on the brink of the subsistence minimum. So how could a small élite get away with appropriating the entire economic surplus? The outward safeguards in the form of the armed forces and the police were not an adequate explanation. The reason was quite simply that the hierarchical structure of society was accepted by a clear majority. A main goal for every governing class is, as Frank Parkin says:

> to make the rules governing the distribution of rewards seem legitimate in the eyes of all, including those who stand to gain least from such rules. The greater the extent to which this is achieved, the more stable the political order is likely to be, and the less need for recourse to coercive means (9).

This is possible in a society where the upper classes have a monopoly of book learning and are in control of school and church propaganda. The stability of the industrial societies of the early 20th century was basically due to the fact that the majority of citizens accepted that 'economic life' followed the inflexible natural laws expounded by the economists, and propagated by schools, and for which the church promised compensation in the life beyond (10).

Therefore, only a minority of the working class backed up the two alternatives — democracy or revolution. Of course, both these demands fell outside the national consensus, as did the

9. Parkin, p. 48.
10. Routh gives an interesting description of how economic doctrines are popularized into downright propaganda. J.B. Clark is the economist who goes farthest in his attempts to bestow scientific legitimacy on the given distribution of national resources. He maintains in a book written in 1899 'that when natural laws have their way, the income accruing to each factor of production is determined by its actual production'. In other words, free competition tends to give labour what labour creates and deserves (Clark, p. 3). Tingsten, pp. 24–32, gives an interesting survey of school and church propaganda for the status quo.

proposals for the right to strike, an eight-hour working day, and the right to paid holidays. But only the small anarchist groups were completely outside the national community of values. They succeeded, however, in showing how vulnerable modern society is to terrorists who stop at nothing (11).

The role of broker played by the government in this hierarchical, stable society was also made easier by the fact that its duties were very limited. Foreign policy, defence, and law and order were the main tasks of the state. Elementary care of the poor and meagre education were usually organized at the local level. The building of roads and railway networks was still mainly in private hands. There was little or no economic policy. The business enterprises themselves took care of industrial policy. Nor had the government any responsibility for employment. In the United Kingdom, for instance, at times of unemployment and weak investment growth, the capital-owning class chose to invest abroad. Gross capital exports amounted to 7 per cent of gross national product for the whole period 1905-13 (12). And the government was not much worried about structural change, which, according to a study by Paretti and Bloch, was much faster at the beginning of the 20th century than during the postwar period, because no powerful section of the upper class was adversely affected (13).

The labour movement emerged and developed during the 20th century. To begin with, its growth had a clearly destabilizing effect. Soon, however, the labour movement began to be integrated in society and took part in forming its dominating values. One milestone was that political democracy came into being and became the very core of a broadened national community of values. Meanwhile, a large part of the revolutionary group joined the reformistic section of the labour movement.

This process could be described in different ways: the labour movement chose the reformistic road to socialism or, if you like, co-operation with monopoly capital. The result is the same anyway. The labour movement became the guarantee against the revolution which earlier seemed so imminent a danger. So, in

11. Tuchman gives a lively account of the terror of revolution these small groups could spread by a few sensational political assassinations and bombings (pp. 73-124).
12. Robinson.
13. Paretti & Bloch, quoted in Economic Commission for Europe, pp. 16-7.

this way, the foundation was laid for postwar stability and the deep-rooted and extensive national community of values (see Figure 2 in Diagram V.1).

The Swedish labour movement, which in a sense typifies this development, was politically accepted during the postwar period, often as the governing party. The democratic tradition formed the framework for the consensus which emerged. The labour movement gained a hearing for the full employment which postwar economic conditions showed was possible. Other demands which gained broad support were social reforms, increased pensions, unemployment benefits, education for everyone, and a more equitable distribution of national resources. The capital owners accepted the trade unions as a historical fact. In return, they succeeded in getting structural change, wage-by-performance systems, and free trade accepted as necessary means for achieving higher wages and a rising standard of living. The right of employers alone to direct and allocate work was not yet seriously called into question although some restrictions were introduced. The situation of the government was changed primarily in that its area of responsibility was drastically enlarged. This was the beginning of the process which has led to today's situation — where the government carries almost total responsibility. But this development was made possible because it took place within the framework of an extensive community of values between a politically involved trade union movement, on the one hand, and owners of capital and business management, on the other (14).

14.The industrial policy programme of the Swedish Trade Union Confederation (LO), 'Co-ordinated industrial policy' written in 1961, sheds a great deal of light on this situation. It says, for instance, that the trade unions want 'the freest possible development — free not only from detailed regulation by the state, but also free from the intrinsic inertia of the system' because this 'benefits the expansive forces and yields the best economic results' (p. 64). The national community of values in Sweden at the beginning of the sixties was probably unique, but many of its characteristics were also discernible in other countries. One possible exception was the United Kingdom, where the trade union movement has never been sufficiently centralized to be able to endorse a national consensus (Pratten, p. 59). One interesting point is that the Swedish trade unions' institutional structure makes it possible for them to take advantage of the national community of values. This is a major reason for their strong centralization. Elander gives a very worthwhile description of the Swedish model. Castles states in a perceptive study of the Swedish political model that 'the Swedish Social Democrats not only share in the ethos of compromise and the search for consensus, but have intensified it until it has become a hallmark of their style of government' (Castles, p. 175).

Outside this community of values, there were of course the constant demands of the capital owners for higher yields on capital and the labour movement's desire for the nationalization of certain economic activities. More important was the growing demand for economic democracy, as yet loosely defined but nevertheless a threat to the sovereignty of business management.

It was, of course, the unique combination of factors sustaining the long and stable boom of the postwar period which made this political and economic community of values possible. During this period *all* groups could year by year get a little more of everything. Also, material values were predominant during this period. People in the active age-groups still remembered the privations of the Depression and the rationing of the war years. Now it was suddenly possible to realize the dreams of modern housing and ownership of a car and a refrigerator.

It was extremely important that the material standard was raised noticeably every year. People's sense of well-being, of a constant, gradual improvement of standard, is psychologically more important than the level of the standard itself (15). The gradual expansion of services supplied by the state, the annual increases in disposable earnings, improved pensions for the elderly, and basic social security for everyone strengthened people's feeling that they were members of a fairly just society. There was a strong sense of being on the right road.

This congenial development in the West European democracies is illustrated in Figure 2 in Diagram V.1. The 'consensus field' is predominant over the conflicting demands.

Standing out in contrast to this harmony, we have today's situation — deliberately dramatized in Figure 3. Many of the factors contributing to this change will be discussed in detail below. At this point I shall give only an outline, sufficient to show how the government's situation has changed.

The picture possibly looks unwarrantably menacing. The parts of the earlier community of values still remaining are qualitatively more important than those which have been lost. The consensus prevailing on the principles of democracy is of fundamental importance, of course. A number of basic rules of honour

15. Scitovsky, p. 138.

such as that agreements shall be kept, honesty, helpfulness, diligence, and society's moral code are all parts of a common culture. But even this social fabric, necessary for all types of free societies, is threatened in the long run (16).

It is quite clear that large parts of the consensus of the fifties and sixties between the labour movement and the owners of capital have disappeared. The trade unions, and also owners of enterprises in threatened industries, are becoming more and more sceptical of the structural transformation of industry necessary under the free trade régime. There is a growing resistance to taylorism and the wage-by-performance system. More and more people are finding the taxation system blatantly unjust, as it actually is, when every year inflation robs the small savers of billions of dollars (17). Owners of capital and business management organize themselves into a front to fight the demands for economic democracy — and some of their pronouncements give the impression that all democracy is called in question. The only economic goals the capital owners and the labour movement agree on are rapid economic growth and full employment.

But even these goals are not entirely undisputed. There is a growing resistance among owners of capital to a policy which guarantees employment, since it reduces mobility on the labour market. The resistance to structural adjustments curtails the prospects of using resources effectively. Also, new organized groups have come into being that are convinced opponents of the growth mania of the consumption society and of the large-scale economies in industry. These groups are as yet only peripheral protest movements with little impact — but they could be the vanguard of a new movement towards a change in hitherto materialistic attitudes (18).

A government can only function effectively if there is a national community of values which is sufficiently durable and sufficiently widespread among the population. There must be certain fixed premises accepted by the nation as a whole if govern-

16. Anell (1978); Crozier et al., pp. 159-61.
17. This development is also linked to an obvious weakening of people's instrumental relation to the activities financed by taxes. See section V.2 for a definition of 'instrumental relation'.
18. See section V.6.

ments are to be able to handle conflicts, no matter whether they do this by political means or via the anonymous market (19). If the national community of values shrinks or falls to pieces, democracy is jeopardized. There is still broad consensus on the principles of democracy in almost all OECD countries. But at the same time there is growing disagreement about the purpose of democracy; what are the common aims democracy should promote? If growing groups of the population find the way society functions unjust and ineffective, then it will not be long before they are questioning the legitimacy of the system. In the long run it is not enough that 'the lack of confidence in democratic institutions is far surpassed by the lack of enthusiasm for alternative solutions' (20).

One of the things that has happened during the seventies is that all interest groups have got themselves better organized in their fight for a share of the common cake. But this cake is no longer growing at the envisaged rate (21). The government quite simply lacks the elbow-room it needs to cope with conflicts. This situation breeds contempt for politicians (22). And it is inevitable that anyone who does not understand the situation the government is in, cannot understand why it acts in the way it does.

But a government cannot govern with elbow-room only in the form of increased resources; it must above all have the ability to implement unpopular short-term decisions and make demands on its citizens. The political margins are often so narrow that governments avoid getting on the wrong side of any interest group as long as possible. Theoretically speaking, this ought not to be a problem. If the government refuses a group certain advantages this means a gain for all the other citizens, and this should

19. Anthropologists have found a few isolated examples of peoples who seem to lack the mechanisms and norms for resolving conflicts. But as a rule practically all societies — both 'ungoverned' and more structured — develop a system of norms which helps them to resolve conflicts and guide the community towards internal peace and stability (Colson, p. 37).

20. Crozier et al., p. 159.

21. Crozier et al., p. 61.

22. I think one can discern a quite shocking contempt for politicians in many economists' treatment of the economic crisis. The kindest explanation of this is that it springs from a lack of insight into the conditions under which politicians work in a democracy where the citizens make demands for which they are not willing to pay.

make the latter more sympathetic towards the governing party. But in practice we have here an exact parallel to the concrete disadvantages and anonymous advantages of free trade (23). The group whose demands are refused is known and can give expression to its justified resentment. But the advantages for other citizens become a homeopathically diluted emulsion.

This inability to say 'No' in a situation when growth is stagnating has a dual effect: inflation and a growing budget deficit. As Michel Crozier says, inflation can 'be considered a direct result of the ungovernability of Western democracies' (24). In the short term, it is the least painful way of solving the problems when strong interest groups want to share a cake which is far too small. As 'resources' have to be obtained by printing banknotes and loans, the budget deficit grows. The most obvious example of the weakened power of governments is that no government in any Western democracy today dares turn to its citizens and ask them to pay for the services they require of the public sector (see Tables V.1 and V.2).

The budget deficit, in terms of its percentage of GDP, has increased drastically during the seventies in all OECD countries. The same adverse trend is evident in net savings in the public sector, probably a better gauge of the problems of financing the activities of society. This net saving fell heavily in all OECD countries, for which statistics are available, during the seventies, particularly during the deep recession of 1974-5.

The public sector

One of the most characteristic features of the modern welfare states is the expansion of the public sector. During the period 1955-76 its share of national resources increased on an average from 28 to 42 per cent in the OECD countries. As far back as the inter-war years, the old 'night-watchman state' had fumblingly started to take on a social responsibility. But not until the postwar period did the dynamic expansion take place. This

---

23.See section I.3. See also Thurow's analysis of the political process as a zero-sum game which means that 'the essence of problem-solving is loss allocation. But this is precisely what our political process is least capable of doing.' (Thurow, p. 12.)
24.Crozier et al., p. 37.

Table V.1   Surplus and deficit (-) in national budgets as percentage of GDP. Four- or five-year averages.
               Current prices

Country	1960-4	1965-9	1970-3	1974-7	1978
Belgium	-2.9	-2.5	-2.8	-4.7	-4.4
Canada	-1.2	-0.8	-1.5	-3.1	-6.0
Denmark	1.1	0.8	—	—	—
France	-1.3	-0.7	3.7	-1.0	-0.8
West Germany	-0.6	-0.6	-0.3	-2.2	-2.0
Italy	-2.1	-3.8	-7.9	-11.8	-15.4
Japan	-0.4	-1.5	-1.1	-3.7	-6.5
Netherlands	-0.6	-2.2	-0.4	-2.6	-3.3
Norway	-1.3	-1.7	-2.6	-4.5	—
Sweden	-0.1	0.9	-2.5	-3.0	-6.8
U.K.	-0.7	-1.1	-1.6	-5.1	-5.2
USA	-0.7	-0.6	-1.4	-3.0	-2.1

Source: 1960-70: IMF (May 1978); 1971-8: IMF (February
        1979). Figures for Sweden from Ministry of the Budget

was made possible by the long boom and the breakthrough of
Keynesian theories.

In many quarters this trend gives rise to fears that the 'productive sector' will become too small to 'support' the public,
tax-financed sector (25). In my opinion, this is the wrong way
of looking at the problem.

Public services — no matter whether they are in the form of
education, the use of roads, or visits to a museum — are goods
on a market in the same way as cars, food, and clothes are. The
difference is that we pay for public services via taxes. This is the
case either because the goods are public, i.e. they must be paid
for by everyone as it is impossible to charge individual consumers,
or because we consider that financing via taxes is a fairer or more
effective method. If all groups in a community are agreed on
the extent, type, and quality of public services and on the fairness
of the payment system, then the problems should be minimal.

25.This is the main hypothesis of Bacon & Eltis.

Table V.2   Net savings in the public sector* as percentage of GDP. Four- or five-year averages. Current prices

Country	1965-9	1970-3	1974-7
Belgium	-0.5	-0.6	-0.9[1]
Canada	—	-1.2	-2.8
Denmark	1.3	3.1	—
France	—	0.2	-1.3[1]
West Germany	-0.6	-0.9	-3.3
Italy	—	-2.1	-2.5
Japan	—	-2.1	-6.6
Netherlands	—	—	-2.1
Norway	—	2.5[1]	0.7[2]
Sweden	—	4.0	1.3
U.K.	—	-0.7	-4.2
USA	-1.1	-1.8	-3.2

*Calculation methods and definitions differ so that caution should be taken in making comparisons *between* countries. Tables V.1 and V.2 mainly indicate the trend for each country during the periods under review.

1) Average figure for 1971-3
2) Average figure for 1974-6

Source: OECD: *Financial Statistics*, No. 11, Part 1 and No. 12, Part 1. Figures for Sweden 1970-7 based on statistics from Ministry of the Budget

The problems of the public sector stem instead from:
— a definite weakening of people's instrumental relationship to extended public activity;
— the difficulty of directing large administrative systems;
— the automatic expansion of spending which is inherent in all protected, labour-intensive activities;
— the role of the public sector in a society where the government finds it increasingly difficult to make long-term rational decisions.
People are consumers of public services in the same way as

they are consumers of goods produced in the private sector, in that they weigh the value of what they get against what they pay — this is what I mean by the instrumental relationship. In the early stages of the expansion of the welfare state there was a very strong positive instrumental relationship. Reforms related to the simple and self-evident — everyone's right to education, children's allowances, pensions for the elderly, and improved medical services. In this stage — which all OECD countries had entered during the postwar period — it was easy to see what you got for your money. Reforms affected nearly everybody and they were felt to be fair and right. Both the average and marginal tax rates were comparatively low for the majority of the population even in the fifties.

Now the situation has changed in practically all respects. The public sector has coped with the simple tasks. Now it has to tackle the increasingly complicated, expensive, and labour-intensive activities — which, in addition, affect smaller and smaller groups. Many people in Sweden who started off working life in semi-serfdom could see their grandchildren studying at the university already at the beginning of the sixties (26). There was no doubt in the minds of these groups that society was becoming more equitable and that you got something for the taxes you paid. On the other hand, the middle-aged man in the street is not so sure today what the improvements are which have caused the real costs of education to more than double during the past 15 to 20 years. Now if you want to know what you are getting for your taxes you have to delve into matters like the teacher:pupil ratio, technical aids in schools, and various kinds of remedial teaching. At the same time there is a growing feeling generally that the quality of education has declined. Nor can the large healthy part of the population who have little need of medical services understand why the costs of public health and medical services have skyrocketed.

A large proportion of increased expenditure in the public sector is attributable to past reforms. We are now paying increasing taxes for benefits we have already come to take for

26.Sweden had a system of landless labourers who were paid partly in kind. This
system was not abolished until 1944, although its practice was considerably
reduced throughout the inter-war years.

granted — public health and medical services, education, and social security insurance (27). Many of the new activities are geared to cope with negative effects — to restore and protect the environment, and to combat crime and drug addiction, which is spreading despite expensive countermeasures.

The general overgrowth of bureaucracy plays some part. When the complexity of an organization increases, the accompanying costs are disproportionately high. Nevertheless it is the inherent automatic expansion due to increased wages and new 'compulsory' activities which weighs heaviest in the expansion of the public sector (28). But there is a feeling that bureaucracy is a parasite feeding on the body of society — and it is the attitude of the general public which is important in this context.

All this definitely weakens people's instrumental relationship to public activity. And at the same time pressure of tax — both average and marginal — intensifies for large groups of wage-earners, highlighting the question of whether the payment system is a fair one.

The basic principle of taxation systems in the OECD countries is that the *proportion* of income individuals pay in tax rises as income rises. But it is doubtful if this is what actually happens in practice. All tax systems have extensive rights to make deductions from the gross income. It is not difficult to take advantage of the system, and tax evasion is certainly profitable if seen only from the angle of the private economy. The community has given many people a good training in the art of getting ahead — and these skills are particularly useful in times of rapid change, inflation, and complex tax and allowance systems. There is no doubt that a growing group of ordinary wage-earners very rightly think that the tax system is grossly unfair. So, of course, they choose their own method for relieving the tax burden — they

27. Many regard the social insurance system as a future problem area (see for example Crozier et al., p. 67, and *West German Outlook*, pp. 56-7). Ladd Jr. estimates that an average American family has seen the tax share of its income increase between 1953 and 1977 from 11.8 to 22.5 per cent without being able to notice any increase in the services it gets. Cf. also Janowitz, pp. 160-1.

28. The costs for the public sector must also include the effects of demands made upon citizens and organizations, e.g. firms' costs for submitting statistics, motorists' expenditure on additional safety equipment, and the costs of measures required for compliance with environmental regulations (Crozier et al., p. 65).

swap jobs (you do my painting, I'll do your plumbing) and work for cash (no bills, no tax-drill). It is quite obvious that a black market for labour has become growingly important in Europe during the crisis. Many who are officially jobless get both unemployment pay and wages for 'black work'. A British chain of department stores recently found that the largest increases in sales were recorded in areas with high unemployment (29).

This state of affairs is due not only to people's instrumental relationship to the public sector but also to the more fundamental issue of the citizens' loyalty to the established order. One basic condition for the preservation of the system is that the great majority feel that, as individuals, they get a reasonable and fair share of the total resources.

The weakened instrumental relationship and growing discontent are contributory causes of the growing budget deficits. Governments' intuition is probably right when they decide not to ask citizens to pay for public services. The tax revolt is most conspicuous in, but by no means limited to, the United States (30).

The task of the public sector is to supply people with the services they need. This requires flexibility and a sensitive ear for changing consumer preferences. Ideally, it should also be possible to adapt services to individual requirements. If decisions can only be made at top level, this means not only that decisions are removed from the level where the knowledge is — with all the information problems this involves — but also that the sense of responsibility and the inclination to take initiative at the local level are reduced. This is particularly important in a market economy where a government subsidy system is on such a scale that firms begin to feel that they can always rely on getting a helping hand from the state. They might even discover that it is easier to get a subsidy than to make an old-fashioned profit.

The administrative system and the market system are two different ways of directing an activity (31). There is absolutely no reason to harbour ideological prejudices about either of the

29. Keegan. See also Freud and Matthews.
30. *Economist*, 23 December 1978.
31. See Vickers's discussion of the economy divided into a user-supported and a public-supported sphere (Vickers, pp. 44 ff).

two methods. Both should be tried on their own merits. A special problem crops up when both systems are used at the same time. Then there is every chance of combining the adverse effects of the two. This is what happens to a large extent when demand is 'socialized'. And this is one of the most characteristic features of postwar development in the OECD countries. By means of grants, subsidies, state development programmes, and general tax allowance rules, the state has created a safe, profitable market for privately owned firms in broad sectors of the economy.

When demand is socialized, its orientation and dimensions change, firms can enjoy monopoly profits, and strong ties are forged to preserve the hothouse climate. The foremost and weightiest example is, of course, the military-industrial complex, which need hardly be commented on. The hotel and restaurant trade is geared to the demand created by the tax-allowance and the expenses-allowance system. In the building industry subsidies, tax-allowance rules and government orders in combination with inflation have led to enormous monopoly profits paid for by the small savers. The profit for banks is guaranteed at so high a level that the market's penalty mechanism no longer works.

Another problem is that a growing proportion of total consumption is taken care of by 'representatives'. The market-economy theory assumes that the person who pays for and uses a purchased product is one and the same — and that he will make up his mind about how he can get the most out of his hard-earned after-tax money. In practice, a growing quantity of goods are bought at the expense of the government, a local authority, or a firm, or they are subsidized via various tax-allowance rules. The person who actually acquires the goods — the tenant with a large housing allowance, the restaurant habitué with an entertainment account, the executive who furnishes his office, or the traveller with a travelling-expenses account — no longer needs to think about the price; he may even think it's a good idea to get as much as possible because it costs so little. Firms get a sheltered market — and it is very much in their interest to preserve the protected area from competition.

A system of government subsidies may be rational from the standpoint of the national economy or of social welfare. An out-and-out market economy in medical services would be regarded as shockingly unjust by most Europeans. Spacious dwellings bring social benefits which the market system cannot measure. The problem is to see through the aggregate effects of government subsidies, for example within one sector. In practice, a subsidy system in, say, the housing market will unavoidably have some obviously unfair effects, which often assume enormous proportions in the public debate. If it is a matter of a temporary demand, there is also a great danger of substantial efficiency losses due to 'false' signals to manufacturers.

It is also important to remember that the public bureaucracy grows because the market economy does not work well and because competition is dangerous. The pharmaceutical firms are careless about product control. After some time has passed, the consequences are discovered. Controls must be tightened and new rules worked out. The result is more red tape *both* in public administration and in the pharmaceutical firms. The building industry uses inflammable materials and hazardous chemical agents; the car industry puts its money into colour and design but neglects the purification of exhaust gases, energy conservation, and safety; the repair firms palm the customer off with botched repairs; electrical goods are carelessly assembled; food contains different kinds of additives. All this means that the community must expand its protective machinery to safeguard the life and health of its members. And these are examples of downright improductive employment (32). It only corrects the mistakes which free competition 'promised' to eliminate single-handedly.

The result of this interaction between growing problems, increasing complexity, higher level of ambition, and an expanded public sector is that the 'system' becomes very difficult to manage or even to oversee. In order to guarantee that all effects are taken into account, more and more institutions – each ser-

---

32. The fact that the public sector is forced to cope with problems which originate in the business sector (retraining, the drawing up of safety regulations, research on toxic products, health care for various occupational diseases, and so on) accentuates the earlier-mentioned differences in productivity. Public activity (whose productivity *is assumed* to be low because it cannot be measured) is a necessary condition for the high productivity of the business sector.

ving a particular purpose, each with its own will, powers, and budget — must be drawn into planning (33). After that, the implementation of plans will affect several different executive bodies at various levels. Bureaucracy is meant to be the government's machinery for carrying out orders, as the military does, in societies with scarce administrative resources. Now bureaucracy is developing into a gigantic body for negotiating and persuading — with no guarantee that the quality of decisions is improved. There is no gainsaying that these trends, together with complicated subsidy systems, 'communal' price fixing and an economy more and more geared to the actions of 'subsidized' consumers, lead to rising inflation (34).

More and more corporations and people are becoming economically dependent on political decisions. This change has several dimensions. As long as the economic sphere is predominant, the government is relieved of a number of problems. The anonymous market forces decide which corporations are to expand and which are to stagnate. The distribution of resources is a result of individual competence, and everyone has to adapt his requirements to his own income. When the political sphere takes over, the conflicts become apparent. The distribution mechanism is no longer a diffuse natural law but resides in interest groups with greater or lesser power.

This brings us dangerously close to a situation where the cause of the social structure becomes transparent, where, according to Weber, the moral foundations of society start crumbling (35). This is one reason why all groups want to keep their privileges a secret. In the United States the paper and pulp industry did a great deal of intensive lobbying *against* federal assistance to local purification plans (36). The reason was that these subsidies would reveal the cost of allowing the industry to pollute free of charge. French farmers were furious when they found out that the subsidies which were paid after a severe drought were to be

---

33. At present twelve different authorities in Sweden have to examine and comment on blueprints for a day nursery.
34. Herin, p. 40; Kristensen.
35. Weber, quoted in Parkin, p. 161.
36. Keegan in Rothschild, p. 149.

financed via a fully visible extra tax (37). But nonetheless we are moving inexorably towards a point where the question of how the resources of society are to be distributed is primarily a political and not an economic one. And, as Daniel Bell puts the question, 'what are the constraints on political demands?' (38).

In this section I have shown that it will be very difficult to solve employment problems by allowing the public sector to expand. In the next section I shall be discussing the serious problem of employment in the whole of the service sector.

The post-industrial society

There is no generally agreed theory on the development towards a post-industrial society (39). But there is one idea which most theorists seem to be agreed on. The importance of the industrial sector will diminish and employment will be increasingly concentrated in the service sector. Daniel Bell is the most explicit spokesman on this point. He holds that a smaller and smaller proportion of disposable income will be used for buying goods:

> Thus, a third sector, that of personal services, begins to grow: restaurants, hotels, auto services, travel, entertainment, sports, as people's horizons expand and new wants and tastes develop ... The claims to the good life which the society has promised become centred on the two areas that are fundamental to that life – health and education (40).

If we look at employment statistics, this theory seems to be correct. In Japan, North America, and Western Europe the number of agricultural workers declined by nearly 14 million during the period 1963-73. Industrial employment went up slightly in the United States and Japan and fell in Western Europe. The biggest increase took place in the service sector with its 30 million new jobs during the period 1963-73 (see Table V.3).

37. de Closets, pp. 178 ff.
38. Bell (1976), p. 226.
39. This kind of society is also called by a number of different names. I have chosen the most common – the post-industrial society. A survey of post-industrialism theorists is to be found in Gershuny, pp. 10-54, and Kumar, pp. 185 ff.
40. Bell (1974), p. 128.

Table V.3   Changes in breakdown of employment by sectors in North America, Japan, and Western Europe 1963-73 (percentage of total labour force and changes between 1963 and 1973 in absolute figures, millions of employees)

	North America		Japan		Western Europe	
	1963	1973	1963	1973	1963	1973
Agriculture	7.3%	4.2%	26.0%	13.4%	15.1%	9.4%
	-1.5 million		-5.9 million		-6.2 million	
Industry	33.0%	31.5%	31.7%	37.2%	43.5%	42.4%
	+4.9 million		+4.9 million		-0.3 million	
Service sector	59.7%	64.3%	42.4%	49.4%	41.4%	48.2%
	+15.7 million		+6.4 million		+8.7 million	

Source: Blackhurst et al.: *Adjustment*, p. 56

But as Krishan Kumar, among others, has shown (41), this is not really a new development. The highly industrialized society never reached the level where the majority of the labour force was employed in industry. Right from the beginning the flight from the countryside meant that employment increased in both the industrial and the service sector. The possibly new feature is that the number of employees is now increasing in the service sector only — and this is mainly due to the far superior improvement of productivity in industry. It is difficult to regard this as a good yardstick of the diminishing importance of goods production.

But what is actually happening in the expansive service sector? What forces will influence developments in the future?

Firstly, a substantial proportion of consumption of services is 'compulsory'. The most expansive 'industries' are schools, public health, and medical services. They account for a large part of the expansion of the service sector both as regards employment and expenditure. The total educational system in all OECD countries

41.Kumar, pp. 230-40.

is the predominant employer, if we take the pupils into account also. Thirty per cent of the United States' total population is today engaged in this field (42).

Secondly, part of employment in the service sector is directly related to goods production. We have transport and distribution services because there are goods to carry and to sell. The banks, consultancy firms, and researchers sell services on a very expansive market — but a great deal of these activities are concerned with the financing of investments in goods production, proposals concerning efficiency improvement in production, and the development of new products. In the public sector also there are a number of activities whose prime purpose is to make the production of goods more effective. One of the main reasons why productivity is so low in the public sector is that it is forced to take over a number of activities from the 'productive' goods-producing sector of the economy. The British economist, Jonathan Gershuny, has estimated that about half of employment in the service sector in the United Kingdom in both 1961 and 1971 was 'goods-related' (43). The fact that increasingly efficient machines and robots take over a growing proportion of the purely physical production, while more and more people are engaged in supervising, controlling, transporting, research, selling, and book-keeping, is no reason for saying that the importance of the industrial sector has diminished.

Thirdly, it is absolutely clear that the proportion of services 'proper' in relation to disposable income — theatre, cinemas, laundry, domestic help, hairdressing, travel — is decreasing. The only exceptions are postal and telecommunications services, and tourism. What is happening is that we are buying machines and producing the services we need ourselves. The private car takes away the need for public transport and taxis. Launderers, launderettes, and the collective laundries in apartment houses are no longer necessary when every dwelling has its own washing-machine. Television supplies an increasing proportion of cultural consumption. Municipal baths are used by the keep-fit enthusiasts, hardly any more for keeping clean. People go to evening classes and buy tools so that they need not pay for expensive

42. Kumar, pp. 248-9.
43. Gershuny, p. 97.

repairs of their cars and heating systems. Ready-made food is mechanically produced to suit the increasingly sophisticated refrigerating equipment in the home. The type of services which involve personal contacts diminish most.

Table V.4   Some expenditure categories as percentage of the total household budget in the United Kingdom 1954-74

	1954	1966	1974
Theatre, cinema, etc.	2.0	1.0	0.8
Television: purchase and rental	1.4	2.1	3.0
Domestic help and laundry services	1.6	1.1	0.8
Household machines	0.8	1.4	1.7
Transport services	3.5	3.2	2.4
Transport equipment	3.5	8.6	11.1

Source: Gershuny, p. 78

The reason is the same as that which makes industry more and more capital-intensive and automated. With present taxation systems, machines are cheaper than human beings (44). We simply cannot afford to buy personal services. The relative costs of these have increased drastically during the postwar period. At the beginning of the fifties, a civil servant or a grammar school teacher in Sweden could buy 1-2 hours of a craftsman's services for his own hourly earnings after tax. Now he can only afford to engage the services of a plumber for ten minutes, and that is not counting the time he has to spend at home to let the plumber in, or the plumber's travelling costs (45). There are several reasons for this: the reduction of wage differentials, the progressivity of

44. The relative costs of labour and capital are increasingly determined by depreciation allowances, tax rebates, personal tax scales, social welfare contributions, and turnover taxes.
45. Figures from the Swedish Association of Plumbing, Heating, and Ventilation Contractors, Swedish Confederation of Professional Associations, and the Swedish Union of Teachers. Gershuny estimates that the price of services rose twice as rapidly as that of goods in the UK from 1953 to 1974 (p. 79).

taxes, 'humps' in the marginal tax scales, social welfare contributions, payroll taxes, and turnover taxes in combination with slow productivity improvement. Trends in other OECD countries are less pronounced than in Sweden, but nevertheless sufficiently clear to explain why the lawful consumption of personal services will in all probability continue to decline — at least as a percentage of the total household budget.

The consequences of this is that people do more and more of their own work — often organized as an exchange of services outside the market — alongside a sharp rise in the amount of receiptless, untaxed trade in services. In the United States it is estimated that non-market work can be valued at nearly 50 per cent of money incomes (46).

What kind of trend can we now reckon with in the service sector? Is it likely that we shall use an increasing proportion of income for buying services? The answer — at least within a given institutional framework and assuming current tax regulations — is probably no. This also means that employment problems will not be solved by a rapidly expanding public and private services sector.

Economic arteriosclerosis

'If any single factor dominated the lives of nineteenth-century workers it was *insecurity*', writes the British historian, E.J. Hobsbawm (47). A worker never knew how long he would be able to keep his job or what he would be earning next week. Unemployment and illness involved downright physical misery and only a few knew how they were going to provide for their old age.

People had to adjust their lives in order to survive. The anonymous market forces moulded their lives. They moved in from the countryside to get jobs in the factories in the towns — and many of them moved on from there to freedom in the New World. Very few could be choosy when it came to the kind of job they did or where they were to live.

46. Scitovsky, p. 87.
47. Hobsbawm (1975), p. 219.

People did not feel that all of this was something they were being forced to do. The towns exerted a powerful attraction. But even so the workers were powerless in the sense that they could not choose between various alternatives. They had to take the jobs they were offered.

This is the situation the organized labour movement had gone out to change in the nineteenth century, but it had to wait until the interwar years before any real progress could be made. The aims of the struggle were higher material standards and greater security. During the twentieth century the labour movement, often in co-operation with liberal parties, gradually built up the social security system. The old poorhouse and workhouse system was replaced by an increasingly comprehensive social insurance system. The financial allowances after tax in some OECD countries are now at a level which makes it possible to maintain the achieved material standard even when unemployed. In some of the rich countries broad political consensus supports the view that social security should also imply the right to stay on in the same area and keep the same job. In the United States, economic security is always given top priority in public opinion polls about desired job characteristics.

This development strengthens the wage-earner's position in relation to the corporations. He can now choose between different alternatives and, above all, he can afford to wait. Put another way — more and more material incentive is required to persuade people to move.

But at the same time as security becomes stronger and more and more comprehensive, material incentives decrease. Only in the United States and in 'less developed' OECD countries are there large regional differences in wage levels. In all other OECD countries, wage differentials after tax for the large occupational categories have been greatly reduced. Also, the general slowdown of expansion during the seventies has meant that fewer and fewer industries can exert a strong demand for manpower.

The development outlined above can be seen from two angles. In economic terms, a firm and extensive welfare network leads to arteriosclerosis in the signals and mechanisms of the system. 'Normal' adjustment mechanisms function less and less well when people do not respond to material incentives. Expansive industries cannot attract workers who do not want to move. Wage levels for most occupational categories are fixed, so that corporations cannot bid sufficiently high. In spite of recession, purchasing power remains at much the same level thanks to unemployment benefits — and, to some extent, to jobs on the side.

A more reasonable way of looking at it is to see the social security network of the welfare state as a response to people's demands. The Darwinist model of the economy is no longer acceptable. Economic policy must be adapted to a world where security, the sense of belonging, and social stability are some of the basic needs.

Economic growth requires a mobile labour market and adjustment to international competition. Security and stability for the individual wage-earner have a price which is paid in the form of a somewhat lower rate of growth. The problem in several industrial countries is that no political party has yet dared to say that this is a choice which has to be made.

There are also a number of other factors which have made the OECD economies more rigid since the war. For example, it is becoming increasingly common for both husband and wife to go out to work. In the United States the proportion of households where both work outside the home increased from 42 to 59 per cent during the period 1958-75. This obviously makes it more difficult to move. The fact that child supervision has to be organized and that children now have more of a say in family affairs also has the same effect.

More and more people own their dwellings. In some OECD countries the number of families with secondary residences is increasing very rapidly. All this helps to strengthen the trend towards greater rigidity.

The government's authority

Among many people there is a nostalgic longing for the good old days. But there is no way back. The old hierarchical order where the word of the government was law and where teachers had authority by virtue of their book learning cannot be brought back. One of the predominant features of development during the twentieth century has been that the authority and status of teachers, in particular, and of the intellectual professions, in general, has declined.

One of the main reasons for this development is the education explosion. The number of seventeen-year-olds going to school in the United Kingdom increased from one-fiftieth at the beginning of the century to one-fourth in the mid-seventies, and in ten years it will probably be more than one-third. In the United States more than 75 per cent of all pupils graduate from high school. The number of university graduates has increased many times over during the postwar period. All important national interest groups now have access to staffs of well-educated experts.

The need to educate was only part of the reason for the earlier extension of compulsory schooling. Its main function, as David Landes points out, was 'to discipline growing masses of dissatisfied proletarians and integrate them in British society. Its goal was to civilize the barbarians' (48). The efforts to get organized among growing groups of proletarian workers constituted a threat to the upper classes. The children of the workers had to acquire the old virtues and respect for the upper classes. School became, and remained during the interwar period, a gigantic propaganda apparatus for the status quo.

During the postwar period the content of education changed in the direction of increased neutrality within the general framework of adherence to democratic principles. At the same time the goal of schools in many countries was to help pupils to be critical and make up their own minds in their judgment of problems.

This dual democratization had far-reaching effects on the authority of the government and of government authorities, since it took place at the same time as the government's broker role was becoming much more difficult. Opinion surveys made in all the OECD countries show a greatly diminished confidence in the competence and honesty of the national leadership. At the end of the fifties about three-quarters of the American people thought that 'in the main, the government worked for

48. Landes, pp. 341-2. The Ragged School Union said in a statement dated 1884 that 'the proletariat may strangle us unless we teach it the same virtues that have elevated the other classes of society'. (Kumar, p. 247.)

the good of the people'. In 1972 only 38 per cent held this view. The majority now thinks that the government mainly works for a few big interests. Between 1966 and 1971 the proportion of the population which had great confidence in goverment was halved. At the same time people are becoming more politically active, and the political scene more polarized (49).

In the European OECD countries also, people have much less confidence in their governments, in government authorities, and in the way democracy functions. And dissatisfaction is greatest among the young, well-educated groups who have lived their whole lives in economic security and acquired the 'post-industrial' values. In Western Europe, too, political activity is increasing in the sense that people organize themselves and try new ways of influencing politics (50). It is no longer enough to vote for a complete political programme once every fourth or fifth year. A new mode of participation is developed which 'is capable of expressing the individuals' preferences with far greater precision than the old. It is more issue-oriented, it aims at effecting specific policy-changes rather than simply supporting a given set of leaders' (51). More and more issues arise on which the voter may be doubtful of the party he traditionally supports. This opens up the way for parties exploiting a growing discontent. It is not a matter of the death of the ideologies that American political scientists dream of — but of a situation where consistent value-systems are disrupted by acute dissatisfaction in particular cases.

There are several reasons for the contempt of politicians which is flourishing in most OECD countries. The 'official' reasons range from political stupidity and corruption to bureaucratic rigidity and inefficiency. But the question is why these sentiments are getting stronger just now. Politicians are certainly not more stupid today than they were before. They are still better informed than the average man-in-the-street. The people in power have always made money out of their position (52). There is a larger bureaucracy than there was before — but there is no doubt

49. Huntington in Crozier et al., pp. 26-85.
50. Inglehart, pp. 142 and 304.
51. Inglehart, p. 368. Also Huntington in Crozier et al.
52. The fact that several members of government and heads of state have been involved in criminal activities — Watergate and Lockheed are the cases that first spring to mind — has of course not improved matters.

that civil servants work harder today than ever before, and often in close contact with the general public.

The most probable reason is that the structure of society has changed. Democracy — the pluralistic society with power and knowledge in many hands — has finally come into being. The number of people with scientific education and competence is increasing. In nearly all areas there are independent and articulate experts who look at society with a critical eye. A particularly important role is played by the 'opinion-moulding industry'. The mass media in the modern society reach practically all citizens several times a day. The focus of journalism is of necessity directed towards the personal and sensational, there is more news about scandals than about plodding work, more about corruption than about everyday honesty, more about crises than about long-range development. The overall picture must become twisted. And people who buy a paper in the streets are often content with something which could be true. The attitude of the population to the government and civil servants must obviously be affected if every day they are told by the mass media that the country is governed by a bunch of fools. It may be significant that the only central institution in the United States whose authority has not diminished is the mass media. Confidence in the credibility of news programmes on television has increased greatly (53).

This situation is made worse by the fact that the political sphere is broadened at the same time. More and more decisions which before were managed by anonymous market forces have now become visible and vulnerable. But the institutions which have to make the decisions can no longer exercise power by virtue of their authority. Truth is no longer unassailable, but something to be negotiated. People's freedom increases. They have different choices and can no longer be commanded. When the hierarchical hegemony crumbles and all questions are found to have two sides, then everything can, in principle, be called in question. There is a clear danger that this development may lead to a flight to ready-made views, to the authoritarian systems we can see on both the right and the left wing.

53. Huntington in Crozier et al., p. 83. The *greatly increased* confidence is probably a short-term 'Watergate effect'.

The changing scale of values

My own view is that a society's system of values and norms develops as an ideological superstructure to the economic structure. But the process is not mechanical. It is an interplay which can either be for the good, that is to say, for the betterment of both, or for the worse, so that growth, for example, is made more difficult by prevailing values. But seen in the long term, economic development is the driving force. Every civilization must adapt itself to its material base (54).

The values which evolved during the postwar period in interplay with the stable expansion were definitely materialistic and conducive to rapid growth. The consumer society was a result of people's desire to get a car, a better dwelling, and machines to make work in the home easier. The democratization of society gave people the right to demand this higher material standard. Technical advances, full employment, and higher disposable income made it possible. Reality became the ideology of the postwar period. And people still cherished the old Puritan virtues of industriousness, conscientiousness, and devotion to duty. They were very much in favour of technical advance — because it gave them the things they wanted.

With the feeble authority of those who are wise after the event we can sit in judgment on this state of affairs. One thing should be borne in mind, however. We cannot make politicians and technologists the scapegoats. The fact is that governments did what the electorate wanted in election after election — they gave priority to rapid technical development which gave better-paid jobs and a higher material standard (55). Of course there were environmental problems early on, but they were invisible, just like the mists over the Thames before Whistler painted it. The spring became silent only when Rachel Carson wrote her book

54. If I am to quote any authority it must be Engels, who in a letter to Conrad Schmidt (28 October 1890) wrote that "the whole gigantic process is developed as an interaction between forces which are admittedly very uneven in strength and where the economic development is the incomparably strongest, most fundamental and decisive", quoted in Kemp, p. 20. See also Marvin Harris's broad analysis in "Cannibals and Kings". It is somewhat pointless to "prove", as for example Lewis does, that this adaptation to material conditions can take different forms (Lewis, pp. 152-196).
55. Anell (1978).

(56). The protests from an increasingly impoverished country-side found no foothold in public opinion. We were the captives of our own vision. There was a symbiosis between our scale of values and economic development. And it takes a long time to get the brakes to bite on a generally accepted development of society.

Since the sixties we have seen a number of new values emerging. Ronald Inglehart calls them 'post-materialistic' in his comprehensive study of changes in value-systems in the OECD countries (57). One thing all these new tendencies have in common — I prefer not to talk about a new coherent system of values — is, as the name suggests, that they are less concerned with material values such as consumption and career. The need to develop one's own personality and aptitudes, to function as a human being and to feel that one is needed in a social context are, according to Inglehart, becoming more and more important. Alongside these tendencies there is a growing doubt about the increasing consumption of non-essentials (status goods) and a definite opposition to some features of industrial development, such as nuclear power and environmental deterioration. Often, growth is regarded as a direct cause of the mismanagement of resources.

These new values have their strongest foothold among young, relatively well-educated people. But the tendencies are not explained by the fact that people are young — it is the social and economic development which has initiated 'post-materialism'. This means — all other things being equal — that the new values will gradually grow stronger. Even today, 'materialists' and 'post-materialists' are equally balanced in the younger age-groups (58).

The explanation is fairly obvious. The young 'post-materialists' have never lived through a depression, war, and poverty. Material standards have been improving all through their lives as though by a law of nature. They take for granted the security and the

56. The first alarm in the environmental debate was sounded by Rachel Carson's book *The Silent Spring*.
57. Inglehart. These issues are also dealt with by Crozier et al., where there is an interesting discussion of similar, although much weaker, tendencies in Japan. Laqueur describes the historical background to today's cultural crisis. For instance, he points to the universal tendency to let today's pessimism form the basis for doomsday prophecies.
58. Inglehart, ch. 2.

well-being their parents have struggled for and at the same time the drawbacks of industrialism have become, if not more apparent, at least more publicized in the mass media.

What we must ask ourselves now is whether these new values have a self-generating force strong enough to withstand economic crises and to influence economic development. There are attitude surveys which indicate diverging trends. The OECD *Interfutures* study shows that materialistic values regained lost territory during the crisis of the seventies. One possible interpretation then is that post-materialism is an idealistic luxury that we have earlier been able to afford (59). On the other hand, Inglehart points out that there are attitude studies which show that these values have a high degree of resistance. The crises of the seventies resulted only in a slight weakening of the new values (60).

If Inglehart is right, this can lead to radical changes in established political patterns. The post-materialists grow in number and thus become politically more important; they are the group which is most dissatisfied with public authorities and the way in which democracy works; they make real efforts to find new ways of influencing developments. They are mainly interested in issues such as the environment, nuclear power, and new lifestyles which are still trying to find their place in traditional ideological patterns, and − above all − their aim is non-materialistic (61). The people who organized themselves politically and brought today's welfare democracy into being had a clear materialistic base. Now, Inglehart says, we are on our way to a situation where 'the relatively prosperous Post-Materialists may . . . comprise the leading center of political dissatisfaction' (62).

Underneath all these post-materialistic tendencies there are a number of conflicts which demand comment. The post-materialists are comparatively better off than the majority of citizens but are nevertheless the most dissatisfied group. This is possibly

59. OECD: *Interfutures*, pp. 99-112.
60. Inglehart, pp. 103-6.
61. There are several examples of political groupings which form around various specific issues instead of in support of recognizable ideologies (see, for example, Crozier et al., p. 87).
62. Inglehart, p. 148.

due to the fact that, on the one hand, they take the material standard for granted and, on the other, the aggregate benefit of having material assets increases much more slowly when the total volume is large. The reason for the latter is that the time at our disposal for consumption, i.e. actually using the goods we possess, is limited (63).

It seems clear that in future the economic system must produce 'goods and services *plus* satisfying social roles' (64). However, movement towards more existential values, with the self-fulfilment of the individual as a central goal, embraces a dangerous explosive force. As long as the fight for a share of the cake is a matter of material assets it is possible, both in theory and in practice, to cope with the problems. Most goods can be mass-produced so that everybody can get a bit more. But if the conflict is a case of individual positions, status, and power, then there is not even in theory an invisible, helping hand. Assets which are limited — e.g. positions in a social hierarchy, status, or top-level jobs — can only be captured from someone else.

Post-materialism arrives on the scene at the same time as we see an increasingly tough manifestation of commercial values. This has to do with changes in the social and physical structure of society. People are forced to move because of structural changes in the economy. The neighbourhood is no longer as stable as it was. Particularly in the rapidly expanding suburbs, where husband and wife both go out to work, people get farther and farther away from one another. The cracks in human fellowship broaden and make way for commercial values where money, and not Man, is the yardstick.

In a close community everybody knows everybody as whole and complete human beings. Love and fellowship are founded on human qualities. The buying of status goods gives rise more to ridicule than to admiration. But in a society where people have little contact with one another the outer insignia take over — the car on the drive, the impressive title, and clothes of the latest fashion. At the same time there is a weakening of the social

63. I have elsewhere used a simple model to show these links between constant time and gain from material resources. See Anell (1978).
64. Harman, p. 29.

controls which guarantee honesty and uphold the virtues which preserve society. This is a threat to the fabric of solidarity which is a necessary condition for people being able to live together (65).

The fact that the clearly materialistic and growth conducive values of the early postwar period have been greatly weakened is also of importance for relations between countries. The general direction of development is much the same in all OECD countries. But the strength of trends varies. There have always been differences in the value systems of different countries, but now these differences, which are of great importance for international competitiveness, have increased.

West Germany, together with Denmark and Ireland, has the smallest proportion of post-materialists of the eleven industrialized countries studied by Inglehart (66). In Japan, which was not included in the study, there are even fewer post-materialists and nearly all of them are men under thirty years of age. The reason is probably a combination of earlier cultural standards and the economic situation after the war.

West Germany was kept in political quarantine for a long time after the war. Economic expansion was practically the only way the nation had of asserting itself. And the dread of inflation amounted almost to panic. Rapid growth and low inflation evolved as overriding national goals. Far into the sixties the trade unions accepted wage increases below the improvement in productivity. Therefore the government could without trouble allow the D-mark to remain undervalued, and this strengthened the international competitiveness of the business sector.

At the end of the war Japan was in the same situation as West Germany. The only difference was perhaps the absence of the dread of inflation — and advantage was taken of this by persuading the small savers to accept low interest rates and so help finance reconstruction. The national enthusiasm for growth and export expansion assumed almost religious proportions. There was and is a strong sense of loyalty and pride among workers in the large corporations, and this has been reflected in practically

65. Anell (1978).
66. Inglehart, p. 38.

no absenteeism by European standards. In the smaller corporations the lack of employment security has had the same effect
(67). Some of the newly industrialized countries — primarily
South Korea — seem to have a very strongly growth-oriented
system of values on the Japanese model.

The old capitalist values are much more pronounced in the
United States than in Europe. Wages reflect the individual's
capability, and help from the State is by no means a given right.
Social reforms which are taken for granted in Europe — national
health insurance, for instance — still meet resistance.

There are several problems associated with the system of
values I have outlined here. The evolution of new post-materialistic values is part of the process which is splitting up the former
community of values. People feel that earlier systems of values
were unfair. This not only splits the frame of reference within
which the government can cope with conflicts — the very legitimacy of the exercise of power is affected. Throughout the OECD
area the multitude of young unemployed is growing — youngsters who can hardly be expected to be loyal to a system which
they have not helped to create and in which they are not needed.

The international order presupposes that participating states
behave in a certain way. Differences in national systems of values
not only mean that states may find it difficult to keep to the
rules of the game, but they also exacerbate conflicts. Countries
with materialistic, growth-oriented systems of values can increase
exports and accumulate surpluses on their current accounts.
This makes the situation even more difficult for countries which
are already 'weakened by post-materialism'.

Justice — an elusive concept

The question of justice has always interested philosophers and,
at times, even economists. Various attempts have been made in
recent years to develop a theory of objective economic justice

---

67. As Bolang has demonstrated, it is a myth that *all* Japanese workers have a safe lifetime employment. This employment security only applies to male employees in
government employ and in the large corporations (Bolang, p. 199). For other
aspects of the Japanese system of values see Pratten, pp. 53-7, and Crozier et al.,
pp. 125 and 147-8.

(68). But here we shall concern ourselves primarily with what people *regard* and *accept* as just. If a democracy is to work, the citizens must have a sense of being treated fairly and of receiving a fair share of the community's resources. The problem is, of course, that this subjective justice is constantly changing. So a balance must be maintained between the actual development of society and people's changing perception of what a just society is.

The old social order, most of which still persisted in the interwar period, rested on the acceptance of an hierarchical structure of society. There was a feeling that those who had power in some way deserved to have it. But this attitude has been weakening throughout the twentieth century. Egalitarian values become gradually stronger and make their full impact during the postwar period. That which was regarded as just at the turn of the century is now regarded as blatantly unjust by practically everyone. The factor which now holds back more radical measures is not values, but the danger of a far-reaching redistribution of income damaging economic efficiency (69).

In the economic field, capitalism is developing into the predominant normative system in the OECD countries. The effective community of values of the postwar period is founded on the fact that all the major interest groups accept the market economy as an efficient way of achieving economic growth, full employment, and low inflation. There is in this consensus an understanding of the need of structural transformation, a mobile labour market, and wage differentials which promote the efficiency of economic activity.

The reason why this system of values is becoming weaker is largely that the way in which the market economy works and distributes the resources of the community is no longer regarded as just. There are several causes for this development, and it is difficult to distinguish between what is actually unjust and what is felt to be unjust. In my opinion, the taxation systems in the OECD countries have, to varying degrees, always been grossly unjust. A combination of liberal tax-deduction rules and inflation means that every year billions of dollars are transferred to

68. One ambitious attempt is Rawls's *A Theory of Justice*.
69. Brittan, pp. 264-5.

the owners of real capital at the expense of the small savers. Diffuse and elastic regulations give great advantages to those groups which have been given a free college training in the art of grabbing. Small firms and the self-employed use legal and not-so-legal loopholes in the tax system to withhold large revenues from the community. In all OECD countries profits made on speculative operations are taxed less than income from employment. This is an actual fact. But the important thing seems to be that these facts are now becoming known in a climate where they can no longer be accepted.

The breakthrough for egalitarian values means that the demands of the worst-off groups become legitimate. They have the *right* to demand a growing share of the cake. The political decision-making sphere is extended. The result is that the market's previously anonymous decisions concerning the distribution of resources now become visible and vulnerable. Top-level employees in corporations cannot defend their privileges on the grounds of their capability when everyone can see that the corporation is keeping its head above water only with the help of state subsidies. When the hand becomes visible one discovers that the money of the wealthy elite was not so hard earned after all.

Once again the mass media play a central role. Existing injustices — those in the tax field, for instance — are brought out into the open and new ones are created. In the fight for news-stand sales of newspapers and magazines half-truths might in fact be better than the whole truth.

Egalitarian systems of values have no break-even point in a capitalist society. The basic principle of democracy is the equal worth of all men — but how can we defend the differences which in fact exist? Welfare policy aims to give more to those who have least — but when do we call a halt? How can we explain that speculative operations are taxed less than an honest day's work? To whom do the profits of a corporation belong when the taxpayers' subsidies to the corporate sector amount to several per cent of GDP? What happens to unemployed youngsters who have acquired the new values but who find that society is hierarchical — and that they are trapped at the lowest level without a decent chance of getting ahead?

The latest conflict between the have-nots and those who control the real and positional values of society assumes a new dimension when the moral basis of the order starts to crumble away. Capitalism has released forces which are becoming increasingly difficult to control. Its first commandment is that everybody shall take as much as he can get, but this is only possible if there is a moral code which lays down the rules of the game (70). It requires a control machinery of totalitarian dimensions if citizens do not have a strong and natural sense of loyalty to a given social order (71).

This is the dilemma of all democratic market economies which have left the hierarchical haven. The new egalitarian values promise an equality which does not exist. The market economy is like a pyramid. Status and social position are by definition limited to the few. You can only get to the top of the pyramid by pushing someone else down. If everyone goes in for advanced education at the same time, it makes no difference to the social hierarchy — it is just as though everyone were standing on their toes at the same time in order to see better. It is possible that all the soldiers in Napoleon's army carried a field-marshal's baton in their rucksacks, but they could not all be the leaders of an army at the same time. You can start with nothing in your pocket in a market economy and work your way up, but only if others still have empty pockets and are forced to sell their labour.

A number of material assets are also positional or hierarchical — e.g. land, places set in beautiful surroundings, antiquities, and status goods. These goods can only be captured from others, they cannot be produced so that all can have a share in them.

The new demands for justice are in conflict with some of the basic conditions necessary for the functioning of capitalism. The market economy cannot keep the promises it makes (72).

The inherent conflicts could be successfully handled during the stable boom of the postwar period. In the fifties want and poverty were still fresh in people's memories, values were pre-

70. Adam Smith, who was a professor in moral philosophy, considered this obvious, but it is usually overlooked in modern economics. (See Hirsch, p. 137).
71. Lasch, pp. 186-8.
72. The consequences of the hierarchical nature of so many social and material values are discussed in Fred Hirsch's brilliant essay *Social Limits to Growth*.

dominantly materialistic, the goal was to give everybody the 'good' life — in the material sense. The demands for greater justice were largely demands for a higher standard of consumption, for social reforms and safe jobs.

It is also extremely important that material welfare gradually improved. The cake that was to be divided grew by 3-5 per cent every year. People's sense of justice and well-being was definitely linked to an annual improvement in conditions. This gave people the feeling that they were on the way to making the grade; a feeling which was strengthened by the fact that the visible attributes of prosperity — the private car, clothes, and entertainment — were being democratized.

The concept of justice changed during the fifties and sixties in pace with the means for realizing it. The sixties were the happily stable period when all trends were expected to continue unchanged into eternity. It was also the time when an increasing number of people organized themselves in the struggle for the cake which would always keep growing.

The generations who have lived through the Depression, mobilisation during the war, and the establishment of the welfare state — they are the unbeatable generations. With their memories of poverty, unemployment, and starvation they could, literally, take part in the realization of their dreams in the fifties and sixties. The leaders of the reformist labour movement saw their visions brought to pass in the social security of the welfare state — made possible by the stable economic conditions of the postwar period. Tens of thousands of today's old-age pensioners were unable, in spite of intelligence and aptitude, to get an education because they could not afford it. Forty or fifty years ago many worked as agricultural labourers with payment in kind on a contract with a stipulated date for moving. Some of them are now living in comfort and security, with grandchildren at university. There is no doubt in their minds — this is the just society.

This is the state of affairs which has suddenly been disrupted during the seventies. Earlier on, it *was* really easy to prophesy the future — you just added on a bit of everything. In the seventies there was a growing sense of genuine uncertainty about the future. In the words of the American researcher, Donald A. Schon, we have lost 'the stable future'.

The crisis is one of accelerating inflation, stagnating growth, and a consequent violent increase in unemployment. It is no longer possible to give everybody a little bit more of a growing cake. Inflation is already accentuating serious injustices in the taxation system. Jobs are threatened, and so calls are made for protectionist measures. The conflict between an egalitarian definition of justice and the way the market economy works is universal and it has gradually been on the way up to the surface. The crisis brings matters to a head.

The present-day younger generation in the OECD countries has very hazy ideas of the depression of the thirties. It has never known what poverty is. Nazism and the threat to democracy are at best historical facts for it. This generation takes the welfare state, social security, and free education for granted. But what kind of dreams can it hope to make come true?

Large groups of young people without hope of getting a job in a society where success is measured in terms of money, where status must be expressed in visible attributes, with no sense of loyalty to a system they have not created, where they are stuck far down in the hierarchy with no honest means of getting what was promised — this is a threat which points to a collapse of the fabric of society (73).

73.Cloward & Ohlin, pp. 106–7.

VI. TOWARDS A NEW INTERNATIONAL ECONOMIC ORDER

> The ceremony of innocence is drowned
> The best lack of all conviction, while the worst
> Are full of passionate intensity
> *William Butler Yeats*

> In doubt his Mind or Body to prefer;
> Born but to die, and reas'ning but to err;
> Chaos of Thought and Passion all confus'd,
> Still by himself abus'd, or disabus'd;
> Created half to rise, and half to fall,
> Great lord of all things, yet a prey to all;
> Sole judge of Truth, in endless error hurl'd;
> The glory, jest and riddle of the world.
> *Alexander Pope*

The sustaining ideas of the postwar capitalist international order grew out of the experience of the depression in the thirties. The power base was a result of the economic and political upheaval of the Second World War. A stable system of rules was supported and held together by national and international factors in propitious interaction.

Was this order unique? Have we, as many believe, just witnessed a 'happy interlude' in the development of the world economy, or can this stable and effective order be re-established? To cast light on these questions I shall try to summarize the earlier reasoning in order to indicate in what environment a new economic order must function.

131

Some vital changes — a brief summary

The old international order, which existed as an idea by the end of the war and was successively established in the following years, rested on the economic, political, and cultural hegemony of the United States. Its system of rules was accepted by the other leading industrial countries. The order was developed by, and for, a small group of industrial countries which entirely dominated the economy of the capitalist world. The situation has now radically changed — and will undoubtedly continue to change.

At the end of the war and in the early postwar years the United States accounted for almost half of the world's total industrial production, and possessed three-quarters of the gold reserves and half of the shipping tonnage. At present the American share of industrial production is well below one fourth. The USA has the largest foreign debt in the world and can compete for maritime freights solely through enormous federal subsidies.

The entire OECD area now accounts for about 60 per cent of the world's industrial production. The share of the developing countries is 10 per cent — and will increase, perhaps be doubled, by the turn of the century. In several sectors companies based in developing countries may assume leading positions on the market.

At the end of the war the United States had a monopoly of the Bomb. It established itself as the absolute guarantor of the security of the western world. The US marines intervened in Lebanon and the Dominican Republic, the CIA organized and supported _coups d'état_ in Guatemala, Iran, and Brazil — and this system was accepted and approved by almost all West European governments regardless of party label. When the Vietnam war was drawing towards its close, there were still few OECD governments that raised any objection to the American intervention.

Confidence in this security system has now been seriously shaken. Nuclear technology is spreading to increasing numbers of Third World countries. Military instruments of power are becoming increasingly blunted (1). The marines can no longer guarantee law and order in the Third World and there is hardly

1. Tucker (pp. 81-3) points out that both military and economic instruments of power have been devalued in the postwar period.

anybody who believes that the United States could defend western Europe against a communist nuclear attack (2).

There is no longer an American hegemony as a foundation for the international order. The world consists of more than 160 sovereign states. The developing countries have an 'automatic' majority in the UN. Many problems, for example those relating to energy, foreign exchange, security, and stabilization policy, can only be solved in co-operation between industrial countries, the East European states, and developing countries.

A future international order must be multilateral — and it is not merely a question of spreading the power among several hands. We can no longer assume that the order can build upon a common frame of reference shaped by Anglo-Saxon culture and Roman conceptions of justice (3). It is becoming increasingly clear — and this is a fundamental change — that a future international order must be based on co-operation between several parties which clearly differ as regards profane ideology, religion, conceptions of justice, and general systems of values and norms.

Another important change is that the expansive forces in the OECD area are becoming successively weaker. The reconstruction phase terminated in the fifties. Housing construction attained its peak in the sixties. The markets for automobiles and consumer capital goods are becoming saturated. Since the end of the sixties OPEC, the other developing countries, and the East European states have grown in importance as buyers of OECD's industrial production. In the matter of advanced capital equipment, the OECD countries now assign well above half of their exports to the remainder of the world. And all this happens when the era of cheap energy abruptly comes to an end.

At the same time the simple means for increasing productivity have been expended. Admittedly, people still move *from* agriculture, but no longer to highly productive industry; rather, to the service sector. The possibilities for Western Europe and Japan to increase efficiency by copying American technology have

2. Kissinger has stated in a speech which, at least in Sweden, has received very little attention that the assurances which the United States regularly gives to its NATO allies are quite simply a bluff and that they had better realize this, the sooner the better. Kissinger declared that he would naturally not have said this if he were still Secretary of State. (Kissinger, 11 September, 1979.)
3. This problem is specially emphasized by Vickers (p. 176).

been largely exhausted. There is an increased uncertainty both about what products are worth investing in and about technical methods for increasing productivity.

The international order which started to take shape during and immediately after the war was characterized by great stability at a very early stage. A largely foreseeable development towards ever decreasing barriers to trade started as early as the forties. The goals in the monetary field were formulated in the IMF Articles of Agreement and the plan began step by step to be put into effect during the fifties.

Now uncertainty and pessimism prevail in many fields. Protectionism has gained ground during the seventies. The OECD governments obviously wish to preserve free trade, but it is uncertain whether they really can prevent a trend towards increasing trade obstacles. Several governments pay lip-service to the blessings of free competition at the same time as they make liberal use of anti-dumping legislation to prevent imports and protect domestic producers. The system of fixed exchange rates broke down in 1973 and the discipline, which in the sixties helped to hold back inflation, thus disintegrated.

The stable sixties, when all trends were extrapolated into eternity, were succeeded by the uncertainty and deepening pessimism of the seventies, when not even the direction of changes could be foreseen. The results of this atmosphere of crisis are noticeable in several fields. Firms are becoming more defensive. Investments fell heavily in the mid-seventies, and minimization of risk is becoming an increasingly express aim. Investors are abandoning stock markets in favour of bonds, gold, and real estate. Research is becoming less aggressive. The planning horizon is shrinking.

If one measures solely in aggregated terms, the world economy in the sixties attained roughly the same degree of internationalization as in the period before the First World War. But in practice it is now a matter of an entirely new kind of international interdependence. Today there are extremely few market activities outside the public sector that are protected against international competition. International enterprises span the whole world. No production of commodities takes place far away from a global distributing and marketing network. The national capital markets are linked together into an organic unit. Services of different kinds — licences, patents, management contracts, technology, and know-how — everything becomes goods on an international market. In this increasingly fine-meshed fabric, reflexes become quicker and quicker. Important technical changes, large purchases of a particular raw material, failure of crops — all have consequences which spread throughout the system. Monetary policy in many countries is more a reaction to external impulses than the result of national planning. Stimulative measures can often not relieve unemployment before growing external deficits and inflation force the government to beat a retreat.

During the sixties a number of 'beneficent circles' between international and national factors were strengthened. A consensus existed also between people's goals and the direction of, and the opportunities offered by, the economy. The generation which, with memories from the Depression, had just experienced the Second World War had predominantly clear material goals in life. Dreams of a centrally-heated flat, a car, and a refrigerator were now to be realized. The new technology was accepted as a means to attain the goals on which all were agreed. Industriousness and honesty were still elements in a generally accepted moral code — and there was work for all who wanted it. In the West European countries especially, such a stiflingly strong consensus was established that the political scientists believed ideologies to be dead. It was the long boom period that made this development possible. Every year all received their share of the growing cake — and nobody had really time enough to observe how big was the *relative* share. Growth provided resources and Keynesian theory the scientific legitimacy for extending the public sector. The welfare state came into being during the postwar period — and it started with the simple, obviously necessary reforms desired by all.

Even during the stable boom period, however, governments avoided some of the structural adjustments which were demanded by the rules of the game. As long as resources were increasing quickly and steadily, it proved quite possible both to have and to eat one's cake. Successive social security reforms, however, became increasingly precise. It was not a matter merely of an acceptable standard of living, but also of the right to get a job in the vicinity of one's home. This is what people as political consumers demanded and obtained. Economically speaking, this was a radical change. Capitalism presupposes, as Max Weber points out, not only that people sell their labour but that they are forced to do so (4). Social welfare aspirations put spokes in the economic wheels. Adjustment mechanisms were weakened and state subsidies increased, since structural changes were no longer accepted. The arteries of the economic system started to harden and this became manifest in the recession of the seventies — but by then a quick return to a more traditional adjustment policy was politically impossible.

More and more groups organized themselves in the struggle for the common cake, almost all with access to their own experts. People's instrumental relation to the public sector was radically weakened. New groups of electors with post-materialistic values perhaps heralded a new, less stable political pattern. Governments' room for political manœuvre, whether measured in real resources, authority, legitimacy, or power, is now constantly shrinking. They lack power to distribute the resources *within* given frames and to induce their citizens to accept rational long-term solutions. The result is rising inflation and growing budget deficits.

As the American political scientist Samuel Huntington points out, it is not certain that a strong government will be internationalistic, but a weak one definitely cannot be so (5). The problem in a nutshell is that weaker and weaker governments are faced with ever greater, more numerous, and more complex problems. If a country is to participate in an international free-trade order, its government must have the authority and power to win acceptance for the requirements of structural adjustment. But the better the order functions, the more probable it is — at least, in a small country — that the government's autonomy and authority will be undermined.

Threats to democracy

The present crisis concerns not only the question of the inter-

4. Weber, p. 207.
5. Huntington in Crozier et al., p. 105.

national economic order. In their extension, current trends towards increased instability concern both the national democratic order and international security (6).

The factors I have touched upon can quite easily be linked together in a negative spiral: to some extent this process is already happening. There is no difficulty in adding new links to the chain leading from today's instability — via growing pessimism and uncertainty, raised risk premiums, and diminishing investments — to falling production. It then becomes even more difficult for the government to keep the demands within given limits. More banknotes are printed to help solve the problems, and inflation accelerates. This adds to the inequality between the small savers and the well-to-do, between the economically weak and those who have received a free college education in the art of getting ahead. But inflation can no longer conceal the rules of the game. The mechanisms of power become more and more visible. More and more people begin to ask whether they are really getting a fair share of the national cake, whether their eight-to-five grind is really properly rewarded. At the same time people's instrumental relation to the public sector continues to weaken. 'Ordinary wage-earners' are becoming increasingly doubtful about whether their taxes are giving them their money's worth. The destructive effect of hardline individual profit-and-loss thinking is penetrating social crevices which grow in societies in which people are getting farther and farther away from one another. When people discover that honesty does not pay off in the long run, it does not work in the short run either.

What has happened primarily so far is that the authority of the government has been undermined. The democratic rules of the game still have a widespread and firm support. But they must function effectively and fairly to be accepted in the long run. If the present trends continue, it will merely be a matter of time before groups of citizens ask *why* they should play the game. And the very foundation for the government's exercise of power will then be at stake.

There are already parties of discontent in stable democratic

6. Regarding threats to democracy see, e.g., Crozier et al. (pp. 2 and 8-9); Bull (pp. 257-8); and regarding the decay of the national state Bull, p. 267, Brittan (p. 247), and Huntington in Bell (1968), p. 316.

welfare states like Denmark and Norway. But in other countries as well there are large population strata that can become the breeding-ground for political unrest. The former middle class — small entrepreneurs in handicrafts, trade, industry, and transport — often with little political thrust, feel themselves threatened by structural changes and unappreciated by a growing bureaucracy (7). Large groups of intellectuals see their dream of status vanishing, and seek a higher object in life. (Nazism was indeed not only the threatened and isolated middle class's alternative to liberalism (8). The Nazis were in the majority at many universities before Hitler's take-over of power (9).) Large sections of the working class begin to feel less at home in their traditional parties, in which young, well educated post-materialists are increasingly taking the lead.

The threats to democracy are real, and this fact must have a decisive influence on the policy of the OECD countries. The economic order must be subordinated to the demands for the preservation of a free social system. This implies, among other things, that government and other democratically elected bodies must preserve means to meet the growing demands made by the citizens. It is doubtful, therefore, if we can accept further reductions of the autonomy of governments — at least as long as there is no radical change in people's demands and values.

Prerequisites for an international economic order

Practically all economic analyses of present problems contain more or less clearly expressed recommendations aimed at preserving or re-establishing 'the good old order'. It is also clear that the OECD governments wish to create a stable and effective free-trade order. Let us therefore see what the prerequisites are for this.

I have already touched upon some of them. The order must, for example, be multilateral, which in the first place presupposes

7. Allardt, p. 207.
8. Seymour Lipset stands for the conventional analysis when he says that 'classic fascism is a movement of the propertied middle classes, who for the most part support liberalism' (Lipset, p. 174).
9. Inglehart, p. 112.

acceptance of this fact itself. At the same time the rules of the game and the decision rules, to be effective, must be in line with the actually existing distribution of power. It is the 5-7 major industrial countries that will be predominant also in the new order — but they cannot maintain it without co-operation with other countries.

There is no scope for any new and lofty goals. The demands as to how the order shall function must be modest; wishful thinking is out. The principal goal must be to accomplish a stable order that functions. Most of the postwar economic co-operation has been negative; its aim has been to remove obstacles to the flow of goods, investments, and capital movements. When it comes to constructive co-operation for the creation of institutions and agreements for economic co-ordination, the only tenable example is the EEC (10). There is no indication that any country is at present prepared to accept a global supranational authority with powers of sanction.

But how then is the order to be maintained? A multilateral economic world order can only remain in being if all of its more important participants observe rules of conduct. It is, for example, desirable that the mature industrialized countries strive for a balance in their external economic relations. It is equally important for states to agree on an acceptable rate of inflation and restrict free-riding in the field of trade. All important agents must — voluntarily or by compulsion — conduct their affairs in the knowledge that it is a matter of 'producing' an international collective commodity without a supranational authority being able to exercise control and demand payment. Each of the OECD countries is probably willing to observe the rules — but only on the condition that other countries do the same. If the tyranny of small decisions holds sway, the order will fall to pieces. So the question is how the necessary co-ordination can be brought about.

Unfortunately it is not merely a technical problem. The OECD countries have in fact greatly differing views on the balance between inflation and stimulation of employment, on the shape of economic policy, and on the future monetary system. Even

10. Gordon & Pelkmans, pp. 97-9.

within the EEC different philosophies exist as to how co-operation between states should be brought about.

One must also ask what price in terms of security policy the United States is prepared to pay for a future stable order, (11) or whether Washington, with the present political system, can participate at all in an interdependent world order. Will Japan be able to manage without a free ride?

All of these problems should naturally preclude any plans for supranational powers of sanction. At the same time good will, altruism, and self-interest hardly suffice to hold together a multilateral economic order. The necessary discipline, co-ordination, and restraint can hardly come about without clear rules and certain international coercive measures, such as an agreement empowering the International Monetary Fund to impose penalties on countries which have too large, 'unmotivated' surpluses in their balances of payments (12). GATT's enforcement function must also be strengthened. Above all it is necessary to keep an eye on governments' increasing use of anti-dumping actions as a pretext for curbing imports. Another possibility is that the fundamental free-trade rules are affirmed in a convention and ratified by the parliaments of the participating countries. This would increase the legitimacy of free trade and enable weak governments to enforce the necessary discipline by reference to 'international law'.

International co-ordination of the demand management is desirable, as also is a common programme for curbing inflation. But it is doubtful whether this can be discussed within the limits of the practically possible. As I have said, countries have distinctly different views on the priorities of economic policy. Nor is there any longer a definite theoretical basis for the shaping of economic policy. What we can hope for is the co-ordination of stabilization policy enforced by the imposition of penalties on surpluses in the balance of trade and on current account.

Some kind of informal co-ordination of demand management

11. Hudson (1977), pp. 113-5 and 143-60; Kolko, p. 201; and Kreinin, p. 314. Hoffman presents the arguments why the United States should accept and adapt to the emerging pluralistic world order.
12. This was originally proposed by Keynes on the eve of the Bretton Woods negotiations, and about twenty years later by the Americans in the Volcker Plan (Solomon, p. 242).

may be possible, however. After all, the record for the last couple of years is in this respect not too bad. In 1978 West Germany, Japan, and Switzerland were running gigantic surpluses on current account; in fact their combined surpluses were many times greater than those of the OPEC countries. However, after the Bonn summit in July 1978 among the seven leading industrialized countries, West Germany and Japan increased domestic demand and their surpluses started to diminish rapidly. At the same time Great Britain, France, and Italy, previously in deficit, were moving into balance. Thus, as Denis Healey has reminded us, 'by the beginning of 1979 the industrial world was moving towards adjustment' (13). This venture in international co-operation was only partly intentional, and the emerging results were nullified by the subsequent rise in oil prices. Nevertheless it proves that there is at least a potential, not only in theory, for dealing with the problems which will dominate the first half of the eighties. As a result of the 1979 oil-price rises the financial surpluses of the OPEC states will increase dramatically. For the years 1980-2 these countries will have an aggregate surplus on current account of $ 200-250 billion. Against this stands the corresponding deficit of the remainder of the world, fairly evenly divided between OECD countries and oil-importing developing countries.

The situation is in principle the same as during the 1974-5 oil crisis. But in practice it is now much more serious. Then there were many developed and developing countries which could and wished to set their sights on expansion. By virtue of a reasonable creditworthiness they could finance their deficits on current account by commercial loans. The transnational banks did not need to draw upon their safety margins when making massive loans to the developing countries (14).

In all of these respects the situation has changed radically. The OECD countries enter the eighties with the express aim of combatting inflation and restoring external balance, which is to be achieved by increasing exports. Few developing countries can raise large new loans, and the banks have started to discuss 'a

13. Healey, 'Oil, Money and Recession'.
14. See p. 77.

jointly organized private international safety-net' (15). At the same time it is obvious that the oil price is being kept down to the present level only because Saudi Arabia has increased its production. There is therefore an evident risk of production cutbacks and new increases in prices. Retaining oil in the ground is at present the best way of preserving its real value.

We thus see that two of the central problems — the uncertainty about the price of oil and the financial imbalance — are directly dependent on some form of agreement between OPEC and OECD.

It is the ability to cope with these short-run problems that determines the long-run possibility of establishing a stable world order. Thus it is long overdue for OECD governments to take a serious look at the demands and objectives of OPEC (16). So far the industrialized countries have not been able even to develop a comprehensive energy conservation policy (17). And the only way to make it attractive for OPEC to keep up production during the transition away from oil is to enforce such strict conservation measures in the industrialized countries that a falling future demand for crude is almost certain.

The tentative discussion in the following section is based on the assumption that some kind of *modus vivendi* between OECD and OPEC will evolve. If this does not come about, there is a risk that at least the more optimistic speculations will be of comparatively little relevance.

An entirely fundamental prerequisite is, finally, that *all* major countries have a common interest in a stable and functioning free-trade order in the capitalist part of the world. Today, on the whole, they do have a common interest. In the OECD it is quite clear that the governments wish to have stable free trade. The goal of the East European countries, as defined by the

15. Stewart Fleming, 'Call for banking safety net'; and Cathryn Davies, 'Warning on bank recycling role'; both in *Financial Times*, 4 June 1980. A more profound analysis of the international loan market will be found in Engellau & Nygren.
16. It is of course simplistic to talk about OPEC as a monolith. Nevertheless it is possible to single out a few demands which are supported by almost all OPEC governments: a scheme to guarantee the real purchasing power of oil revenues, transfer of technology, industrial co-operation, and 'political aspirations'.
17. The International Energy Agency has, for example, recently published a forecast which indicates a continuing increase of oil requirements in OECD countries.

Soviet Union, is primarily a *status quo* in security policy and this is considered, at least in the present situation, to be promoted by continued free trade in the capitalist sphere. The Chinese, during the Maoist era, spoke out in favour of an increased international disorder. Now, however, China has joined the conservative forces. The newly industrializing countries have everything to gain and nothing to lose from well functioning free trade. Within OPEC there are some members who actively support a development towards increased instability, but most oil-exporting developing countries are definite advocates of law and order.

We may recognize that all major countries and most of the others wish to have an international order in which the OECD countries preserve an open and stable free-trade system — the question is whether this is possible.

Future options

'If I were to go to Banagher,' the Irishman said to the inquiring traveller, 'I would not start from here.' The same applies to the creation of a future international order. We should naturally have started in the sixties, when everything was possible.

To use a hackneyed phrase, it is difficult to prophesy — particularly about the future. But that is not true. Only 15-20 years ago it could be done very well. In the sixties the future was quite simply a little more of everything — higher salary, larger dwelling, rising productivity, longer holidays, more exports and imports (18). Now there is a genuine uncertainty and a growing pessimism about the future. The word 'development' is beginning to have a threatening note. Earlier generations could live in a stable economic and social environment. Now important aspects of our cultural environment are changing in a person's lifetime. Our children enter into a new world. They are the guinea-pigs of our own development.

'The unbeatable generations' — those who experienced the years of want and war and whose dreams were realized in the security and material standard of the consumer society — are now being succeeded in working life by the first postwar generation.

18. The best summary of the golden sixties will be found in Pollard.

For these young post-materialists welfare is something that is taken for granted. Growth has had its day as a secularized religion. An economic crisis which calls for a national mobilization *may* fill existential voids.

The problem is roughly this. How can the governments of the OECD countries manage to maintain the democratic order, create meaningful employment, and at the same time preserve or re-establish an effective and stable international order? What form should such an order take if it is to be compatible with the demand for sufficient national autonomy? Are there realistic alternatives to continuous efforts to adjust to an international free-trade system?

The coming years will probably be characterized by short-term solutions and compulsory adjustments. There is every indication that economic growth will be lower and less stable than in the sixties. There are no signs of a speedy improvement in international co-operation between the OECD countries. We shall slowly drift into a situation which, in the words of Assar Lindbeck, may be characterized as 'semi-organized anarchy' (19).

This situation is untenable, however, even in the fairly short term. The chief reason is that the allocation of national resources is primarily governed by negative criteria. It will be the problem sectors that secure a disproportionately large part of the nation's administrative capacity and financial resources. And even if it is accepted that the state controls investments, it is unreasonable to take the *non-competitiveness* of companies as a guide in deciding how and where to allocate resources. It seems clear that both a brutal policy of adjustment and a planned partial retreat from the international economy would in the long run be more rational solutions than the stopgap policy now being pursued in several OECD countries. Let us therefore look a little at these two alternatives.

The economist's solution

There is 'little reason for growth pessimism . . . at the purely economic level,' write the economists Richard Blackhurst, Marian

19.Lindbeck in *From Marshall Plan*, p. 85.

Nichols, and Jan Tumlir in an intelligent and eloquent defence of the free-trade alternative. 'The difficulty lies at the political level' (20). If only this obstacle can be removed, there will be no difficulty in dealing with employment, inflation, and competition from developing countries, and in increasing investments. 'All these problems have one and the same solution which consists of making the structure of production in industrial economies more flexible' (21).

This is 'the economic solution' — hard-fisted adjustment to the rules of the game of free trade. Most of the consequences of such a policy can be foreseen. Both in the goods and the services sector, internationalization will continue. Viewed as a whole, however, the pace may diminish, as the services sector — the degree of internationalization of which is, in absolute terms, low — will continue to increase in relative importance in the OECD area. The newly industrializing countries will increase their share of the world's industrial production both by dint of their own exertions and owing to the way the transnational companies organize their production chains.

The crucial gain for the OECD countries is a material one. The total production of goods and services, as reflected in national accounts, will be greater than in other conceivable alternatives.

We assume that more material resources are better than fewer — other things being equal — and that there is a positive relation between a good economic result and a sound situation in the community in other respects.

Compared with other social sciences, economics offers a model of superior logical structure and consistency. This is both a strength and a weakness. The main weakness is that it is difficult to see the problems: the internal consistency of the model means that the solution is always at hand. There are actually never any economic problems. The problems are always 'at the political level'.

The economic solution entails above all two 'political' problems. They are associated with the effects of structural change and with national autonomy.

20. Blackhurst et al., *Adjustment*, p. 67.
21. Ibid., p. 69.

A continued quick structural transformation of international conditions will in several respects have worse effects in the OECD countries than it had in the fifties and sixties, when weak companies collapsed while at the same time new jobs were created in expansive sectors. Much of the structural transformation that took place was made possible by people's willingness to move to other places, to more secure and better-paid jobs. Most observers do not now believe that the OECD countries will be able to attain full employment before the 1990s, and that in several regions the economic structure will be close to the critical limits for survival. Furthermore, competition with the newly industrializing countries will make the structural transformation increasingly horizontal; it will affect entire branches of industry and no longer only a single sector or single company. There is now an urgent need for structural reorganization in the OECD countries.

Continued internationalization will further curtail governments' margins for action. To compensate for this, free trade promises a quick increase of real resources. But the material gains from free trade have in all estimates proved to be surprisingly small (which is not to say that a development towards greater autarchy may not be very costly). The increase of resources is also subject to the eternal law of diminishing marginal return; 'economic gains became relatively less important, particularly to those segments of society that had never experienced severe economic deprivation' (22). Another problem, revealed in Allardt's study of welfare in the Nordic countries, is that compensation for deficiencies in (for example) human relations or social identification can to only a small extent be gained from greater supply of material resources. Welfare policy must be multi-dimensional. 'All social objectives demand their particular concern and their specific policies to be achieved (23).

It seems clear that the purely economic solution can be achieved only in parallel with a change of people's values. Postmaterialistic demands must give way to allow the outcome of the market forces to be the guide in the national allocation of

22. Inglehart, pp. 285-6.
23. Allardt, p. 181; concerning 'compensatory consumption', see pp. 39-43.

resources. Among both governing and governed a renewed and reinforced confidence in the efficiency and legitimacy of the market mechanism is needed. Without such a resurrection of 'the old creed' there is no chance for governments to exercise the discipline required for acceptance of the structural adjustments imposed by an international free-trade régime. Probably, too, the present trend towards a more profound and decentralized democracy must be arrested. It may be necessary to return to a more strictly representative democracy in which strong governments are held accountable only every fourth year or so. This solution is not impossible — perhaps not improbable — even if it entails, for instance, a conscious acceptance of 'peripherization' of regions and groups of people. History (which is as usable as statistics when something is to be proved) shows that the majority often choose order in preference to freedom.

The economic solution, however, is not without its dangers — the threats to democracy are real — and there are no guarantees that even the technical means are available to maintain a stable free-trade system.

The non-existent alternative

In view of the difficulty of maintaining a stable free-trade system it would seem natural at least to discuss possible alternatives. But, with some few exceptions, there is hardly any discussion going on involving governments. The world economy has attained such a degree of internationalization that the possibility of opting out does not appear realistic. The economic model has so stifling a hold that not even partial trade restrictions can be discussed. In a certain sense, too, free trade is the only order that governments can strive for. Economic science shows that free trade across national frontiers is the most effective way of allocating the world's resources. All other orders, in this perspective, are imperfections. No established theory exists in the OECD countries for alternative ways of organizing production.

Even if the world's governments continue every day to make decisions which restrict trade, we may be quite sure that within the foreseeable future there will be no negotiations for an ordered retreat from free trade. And it is not a matter of a double standard of morality. The OECD governments really wish to attain the ideal they are constantly forced to deviate from. This signifies that a trend towards more restricted trade will be looked upon as an undesired but inevitable compromise.

It is however worth recalling that we already have a large number of regulations and restrictions in the existing international trade system:

— a large proportion of world trade is strictly regulated by different agreements. A number of primary commodities are governed by price and production agreements. Shipping is regulated through private cartels. The trade in textiles is regulated by the Multifibre Agreement;
— agriculture is largely protected from international competition;
— state trade, barter, and compensation transactions constitute probably a growing part of international trade. Large export deals or civil engineering projects are now rarely negotiated without governments' taking part;
— 30-40 per cent of the world trade in industrial products is intra-firm trade, i.e. organized within transnational companies;
— a considerable part of the OECD countries' exports is financed with tied aid and export credits;
— below the official surface there is a pervasive web of informal rules and regulations governing practically all important markets for manufactures. This system is managed by numerous 'clubs' or 'associations' of the enterprises concerned. The main function is to preserve the existing market structure and accommodate necessary changes in an 'orderly manner'.

An evolution towards more organized markets could thus take place as a gradual change in which already existing regulations are broadened, strengthened, stabilized, and — in some instances — made visible and formal.

It is, of course, impossible to discuss what effects such an evolution might have, without exactly defining its extent. But it must be made clear that the main problem of the present protectionism is *not* that it imposes new obstacles to trade but that it creates uncertainty as to what rules will apply in the future.

It is here that one can distinguish the possibility of an ordered, partial retreat from free trade. The object would be to find a level where a limitation of trade is the price that is paid for a new stability — and even a substantial general increase of tariffs could well be a price worth paying. From the economist's point of view this could never qualify as the best solution; but it could be the second-best-but-only-possible solution. It is therefore unfortunate that OECD governments are ideologically prohibited from contemplating even modest curtailments of free trade.

In terms of productive efficiency there is certainly a price to be paid. Even if all calculations indicate that the gains from free trade are surprisingly small, there could still be a substantial loss when the process is reversed. However, there are also some benefits beside the increased stability. The scope for national autonomy will be somewhat greater if the obstacles to trade increase. Certain domestic branches of production will become profitable again — without for that reason being entirely protected from international competition. Increased tariffs mean that the domestic market gets some protection, but it is still supervised by international competition. Tariffs will also provide a much needed reinforcement of the public exchequer.

No doubt a case could be made for an organized retreat from free trade *if* the alternative is continued or worsened *ad hoc* protectionism.

Another reason for increasing the national autonomy is that it is the most sensible way of making international interdependence amenable to collective management. If mutual interdependence poses a real or imagined threat to vital national interests it will not work (24).

Some vital choices

Neither a stable free-trade scenario nor an organized retreat represents a panacea for the problems besetting the industrialized countries. Stagflation and unemployment will be with us during the eighties whether we choose to regulate international trade or not. Furthermore there are a number of agonizing conflicts to be resolved at the national level, irrespective of the international environment.

24. Hoffman (p. 28) has argued this point from a different angle.

An already existing conflict lies in *the balance between post-materialistic values and economic growth*. The cherished dream of the economist is that everything is adapted so that the *economy* shall function as efficiently as possible. This is the Brazilian solution: 'The economy is doing fine but the people are not' (25). But, of course, a return to the economic Darwinism of the nineteenth century is out of the question. The social security network that has been created is a response to the express priorities of the citizens. The issue now is what role the new post-materialistic values shall be allowed to play. We do not yet know whether they will develop into a new staunch ideology or whether they are a set of luxury opinions we have indulged in during the seven fat years but are now prepared to cast overboard when the lean years come. A foreboding that concerns us closely is that the new values represent a rather basic creed for at least part of the young generation, in the sense that they will pursue qualitative objectives even at the expense of their material well-being. That would imply that there is no clearcut choice between growth and post-materialism.

In which case we can forget the dreams of the economists and focus our attention on the minimum demands. In all industrialized mixed economies, prices and supplies of goods and services are to a large extent determined by market processes. This role must be performed — either by the market mechanism or by something else. As long as there is no alternative, this basic function of the market mechanism must be preserved. This is the minimum economic demand, and implies that the market must be allowed to define certain rules for society as a whole. Thus the market must stake out the lines for society's allocation of resources and indicate the upper limit of what it can afford. The risk in several OECD countries is that the economic mix is becoming so viscous that the market mechanism is no longer able to keep the system moving.

More important still is that Adam Smith's idea of a basic transformation from individual profit-hunting to common good is made to work. The 'system' must therefore quite clearly put a premium on the type of individual conduct that is collectively desirable. Perfect this transformation can never be, but it must

25. Said by the Brazilian president Medici, according to Black, p. 239.

move in the right direction. The threat is that it is now often more profitable to procure state subsidies and look for loopholes in the taxation system than to manufacture a good product.

In theory the choice between rate of economic growth and different forms of quality of life is not difficult. It can be shown how many tenths of one per cent of the rate of growth must be sacrificed in order to increase leisure-time, or reduce the tempo of work or mobility in the labour market. In practice, however, one encounters the problem that too many and detailed restrictions may damage the very essence of the dynamic process — and then there is the risk that even small changes become bacteria which spread disease throughout the economy. Here, accordingly, there is again a limit which must not be exceeded if the market mechanism is to continue to play its role. If governments increase their protection of business enterprises and citizens, they undercut the implicit assumptions of the market economy. Of course there is nothing wrong if economic security is accepted as the principal goal in a democratic society (26) — my point is only that one should be aware of the consequences.

The problem must, however, not be exaggerated. The margins for finding an acceptable combination appear fairly wide. During the twentieth century the market mechanism has proved to be an extremely robust and adaptable device. The minimum demands that have been outlined should be possible to reconcile with quite divergent precepts as to how society should be organized. Optimism on this point is important also because the conflict between growth and values is directly related to the question of the legitimacy of the system. Political democracy is intimately associated with a functioning economy.

Another conflict concerns *the widening gulf between the increasingly integrated economy and the much slower development towards international political integration*. And this problem is aggravated because, as Andrew Shonfield has pointed out, 'international interdependence grows while the notion of international management of the world economy moves into disrepute' (27).

26. Thurow (p. 19) argues that economic security is in fact the principal goal for both individuals and companies.
27. Shonfield, p. 11.

There appears to be no chance during this century that we shall see supranational bodies which can pursue an effective and accepted economic and monetary policy. But this would be the logical sequel to the economist's free-trade solution: to move the political decision-making and 'law enforcement' structure in line with the ongoing internationalization of the world economy. However, if, as I assume, most major decisions will continue to be vested in national governments, this would strengthen the case for an organized retreat from free trade. My own guess is that the differences among the OECD countries on economic priorities will increase, partly in consequence of their different abilities to live in an interdependent world economy in crisis. At the same time countries outside the Anglo-Saxon cultural circle are growing in strength. Both these tendencies point to the need to preserve an adequate measure of national autonomy. There seem therefore to be good reasons for attempting to reduce internationalization of the world economy or, at all events, to arrest the present interweaving of national economies.

It is quite possible that Charles S. Maier is right when he claims that 'the concept of growth as a surrogate for redistribution appears in retrospect as the great conservative idea of the last generation' (28). Nonetheless the classic *conflict about distribution* will be a central one during the eighties — and not only because the rate of growth is slower.

In the OECD countries it is assumed, at least in theory, that private investors will undertake the necessary development of industry. For them to do so, a certain stability and belief in the future are required, and they must also have a good chance of getting their money back with interest. In reality most of the capital for gross investment is generated within companies. However, this 'internal' capital is required to yield a reasonable return.

The profit level for industry in recent years has been low in comparison both with earlier periods and, for example, with fully secure financial investments or speculative gambles. Investment in new industrial capacity is increasingly risky and less and less attractive as compared with other options.

28. Hirsch & Goldthorpe, p. 70.

To get investments moving in the traditional way requires a very considerable raising of the profit level (and thus of the dividend to shareholders) in the corporate sector; perhaps also, guarantees are required against too radical political demands for employee participation. But is this really possible? It would mean a radical change of attitude on distribution issues and a break in the trend towards increasingly egalitarian values — a development that has been going on and has been successively strengthened since the end of the last century.

In any case, it seems highly unlikely that such a radical change will come about only in order to accommodate so comparatively weak and anachronistic a group as the shareholders. It is a long time since their financial contribution to industrial expansion was of any importance. At present their net contribution is quite insignificant or negative (29). At the same time it is becoming more and more difficult to see who has the *moral* right to the surplus. Through state grants, loans, subsidies, tax rebates, tax deduction rules, and support-purchase programmes the citizens already finance large parts of companies' business activities. In research it is not unusual for the state to bear the greater part of expenditure. The workers occasionally 'refrain' in wage negotiations from obtaining the maximum possible, having regard to the company's and society's long-term interests; they thus acquire a moral hold on future profits. Companies can hardly cope with the investments of the eighties on their own unless they can 'finance' them through increased income differentials — and this is politically impossible.

The result of this development will probably be a continued tendency for the production surplus in the private sector to assume the character of public property. This tendency is reinforced by what John S. Goldthorpe calls 'realization of citizenship' (30), i.e. that we have finally reached the point where

29. To some extent this question depends on how pension systems are financed for the main wage-earner groups. In countries where the premium reserve method of insurance predominates, it is not out of the question that higher yield requirements can be accepted, since the dividend increases the income of the pension funds. In countries like Sweden, where pensions are financed on a current basis, there is today quite simply no powerful group which has an interest in high capital yield in the corporate sector. See Calmfors & Wadner, pp. 98-104.

30. Hirsch & Goldthorpe, pp. 201-4.

we are all equal members of the community. When this idea is taken seriously, it can no longer subsist alongside the distribution principles of capitalism.

This trend towards common ownership and responsibility must probably form the basis for governments' attempts to recreate a national consensus. It is not possible to preserve the *status quo* or to resuscitate the former hierarchical system of values. A new stability must build upon new valuations of who owns and administers the means of production.

Ideas of economic democracy naturally create the same apprehensions as the demand for political democracy once did. But opportunities for the working class to participate in and take responsibility for the administration of society did not lead to chaos but to a stability and efficiency greater than ever before. Thus the presence of worker representatives and other citizens on the company boards should not spell doom for industrial efficiency but, hopefully, contribute to a new social and political consensus.

A less obvious but nevertheless real conflict is caused by the *growing tension between the formal and informal sector* in the modern welfare state. There are many reasons for this. Work in the formal, taxed sector is becoming less and less competitive in relation to do-it-yourself-work or employment in the no-questions-asked market. The financial advantage of a short spell in the 'underground economy' while on the dole or receiving sickness allowance is almost irresistible for people who feel the crunch of recession in a society where everyone else seems to be getting ahead.

This is the cost-push part of the explanation for the growth of the informal sector, but there is also a demand pull. Ordinary employees can no longer afford to buy taxed and socially insured services for honestly earned money (31). The demand for cheap, untaxed services therefore rises. Thus the informal sector, embracing everything from pruning the roses in one's own back-yard via neighbourhood co-operation to organized work outside the tax economy, is already substantial. American studies put the value of 'non-market work' at about 60-70 per cent of the

31.See pp. 113-14.

monetary national income (32). If the underground exchange economy is added to this, we may well think of the formal and informal sectors as almost equal in size.

The problem for governments is whether they shall support or oppose the development in the informal sector. Just to let the matter rest is neither reasonable nor possible. At present the situation in some OECD countries is that small companies in the service branches are forced into fraudulent evasion of taxes and social charges in order to avoid being priced out of the market. A minimum requirement in a society governed by law would appear to be that honest work shall be, if not profitable, at all events possible.

But there are several reasons for believing that governments cannot compel a strict compliance with present taxation rules. The black economy is already quite large. The possibilities of control are slight, since buyers and sellers have common interests and social control is weak. The potential gains for the evader are very great. In several respects, moreover, the legislation lacks moral support. To consider various forms of neighbourhood co-operation as tax evasion is quite simply incomprehensible to the majority of citizens (33). Only the more organized black-market transactions are thought of as morally reprehensible.

We may thus assume that governments must accept the informal sector as a fact of life. Once it has been decided to legalize different kinds of neighbourhood co-operation, it is important to realize that this can be a very effective instrument for organizing several activities, such as transport, distribution of goods, care of the elderly and of children, repairs, and maintenance. In all these spheres the necessary specialist knowledge exists, amply and evenly distributed among the population. And this makes effective and decentralized co-operation possible, with the added advantage of its being shut off from international competition.

This active development of neighbourhood co-operation also provides a means to relieve the burden on the public sector. This should be possible, since there have never been any technical or logistic reasons for the centralization of welfare policy. The

32.Scitovsky, pp. 102 ff.
33.Organized co-operation in informal guilds was the rule in the Swedish countryside a few generations ago. See Hellspong & Löfgren.

reason was instead ideological: the labour movement wished that all should share in and obtain the same rights. This was only possible in a hierarchical society where the responsibility was placed on a central government authority. The risks of local élites being able to acquire unfair advantages by virtue of an expert monopoly are today far less. If the State lays down minimum standards it should be possible to decentralize parts of the welfare system (34).

One very obvious line of action seems to be to reduce the working week. This would provide employment for more people and allow a 'legalized' informal sector to expand. No doubt the market system would respond to this development by providing an increased output of do-it-yourself equipment, thus facilitating further growth, effectiveness, and institutional options in the informal sector.

Some curbing of the growth of the public sector is probably inevitable. The reasonable course appears to be that this should be effected by decentralization — probably to levels below the present municipalities. Decentralization is, however, no panacea. It appears quite clear, for example, that industrial policies need to be centralized. The relations with the international economy must be handled at national level and combined with more effective control instruments than at present exist in the mixed economies of Europe.

I may be indulging in wishful thinking, but I see it as almost unavoidable to strengthen government's control of the national financial system. A firm command of the domestic financial system and external transactions is a natural first step in a strategy to enhance national autonomy (35).

Whether one opts for centralization or decentralization it is important to define very clearly the structure of decision-making and distribution of responsibility. An overwhelming bureaucratic problem is that so many authorities today must participate in

34. An interesting and perceptive discussion of a 'smaller', decentralized, co-operative Sweden is presented by Akerman (1979).

35. I am in great sympathy with Keynes's statement that it is unreasonable to try to 'maximize economic entanglement among nations. Ideas, knowledge, science, hospitality, travel — these are the things which should of their nature be international. But let goods be homespun whenever it is reasonably and conveniently possible, and, above all, let finance be primarily national' (Keynes, p. 758).

preparing and implementing decisions. The responsibility for drafting, formal decision, implementation, and supervision is often spread over different organizations. The problems increase exponentially when local, regional, and central levels are also involved. Thus a clearcut decision-making process, either centralized or decentralized, seems to have many advantages as compared with the present situation.

There is no ready-made solution to the problems of the welfare state. New experience will be gained from the customary trial-and-error process. But this should lead to one crystal-clear conclusion: the OECD countries should use a far greater part of their financial and human resources to experiment with new and unconventional ways of organizing production, public services, housing, and community relations in general. An enormous potential exists in people's ability and willingness to produce and participate. The tragedy of today's industrailized and regimented society is that this potential cannot be mobilized for the national good, but is nevertheless prevented from being realized on the individual level.

REFERENCES

Agmon, Tamir & Kindleberger, Charles P. eds.: MULTINATION-ALS FROM SMALL COUNTRIES. MIT Press, Cambridge, Mass., and London 1977.

Åkerman, Nordal: GEORGIA. DEN NYA SODERN — OCH DEN GAMLA. Forum, Stockholm 1978.

Åkerman, Nordal: CAN SWEDEN BE SHRUNK? in Development Dialogue 1979:2, Dag Hammarskjöld Foundation.

Allardt, Erik: ATT HA, ATT ALSKA, ATT VARA. OM VAL-FARD I NORDEN. Argos förlag AB, Lund 1975.

Anell, Lars: DE NYA INDUSTRILANDERNA — HOT ELLER LOFTE. Paper published by the Swedish Secretariat for Future Studies 1980.

Anell, Lars: SOLIDARITET OCH KOMMERSIALISM in Tiden No. 9/10: 1978.

Anell, Lars & Nygren, Birgitta: U-LANDERNA OCH VARLDS-ORDNINGEN. Sekretariatet för framtidsstudier, Stockholm 1978. (Now available in English — THE DEVELOPING COUNTRIES AND THE WORLD ORDER — published by Frances Pinter (hardcover) and Methuen (paperback).)

Bacon, R. & Eltis, W.: BRITAIN'S ECONOMIC PROBLEM: TOO FEW PRODUCERS. Macmillan, London 1976.

Barnet, Richard J. & Muller, Ronald E.: GLOBAL REACH: THE POWER OF THE MULTINATIONAL CORPORATION. Simon and Schuster, New York 1974.

Bell, Daniel: THE COMING OF POST-INDUSTRIAL SOCIETY. Heinemann, London 1974.

Bell, Daniel: THE CULTURAL CONTRADICTIONS OF

159

CAPITALISM. Basic Books, New York 1976.

Bell, Daniel ed.: TOWARD THE YEAR 2000. Houghton Mifflin, Boston 1978.

Berthelot, Yves & Tardy, Gerard: LE DEFI ECONOMIQUE DU TIERS MONDE. Commissariat Général du Plan. La Documentation Française, Paris 1978.

Black, Ian Knippers: UNITED STATES PENETRATION OF BRAZIL. Manchester University Press, Manchester 1977.

Blackhurst, Richard; Marian, Nicolas & Tumlir, Jan: ADJUSTMENT, TRADE AND GROWTH IN DEVELOPED AND DEVELOPING COUNTRIES. GATT Studies in International Trade No. 6. Geneva 1978.

Blackhurst, Richard; Marian, Nicolas & Tumlir, Jan: TRADE LIBERALIZATION, PROTECTIONISM AND INTERDEPENDENCE. GATT Studies in International Trade. Geneva 1977.

Bolang, Olle & Rumi: RADD FOR JAPAN? Tidens förlag, Stockholm 1978.

Bosson, Rex & Varon, Benison: THE MINING INDUSTRY AND THE DEVELOPING COUNTRIES. (World Bank) Oxford University Press, Oxford 1977.

Boston Consulting Group: A FRAMEWORK FOR SWEDISH INDUSTRIAL POLICY. Appendices 7-11. Liber Förlag, Stockholm 1979.

Brittan, Samuel: THE ECONOMIC CONSEQUENCES OF DEMOCRACY. Temple Smith, London 1977.

Bull, Hedley: THE ANARCHICAL SOCIETY: A STUDY OF ORDER IN WORLD POLITICS. Macmillan, London 1978.

Calleo, David P. ed.: MONEY AND THE COMING WORLD ORDER. New York University Press, New York 1976.

Calmfors, Lars and Wadner, Goran eds.: SVERIGES EKONOMISKA KRIS — BLANDEKONOMI VID SKILJEVAGEN. Natur och Kultur, Stockholm 1980.

Carson, Rachel: TYST VAR. Prisma, Stockholm 1979.

Castles, Francis G.: 'Swedish Social Democracy: The Conditions of Success' in POLITICAL QUARTERLY Vol. 46 No. 2, April-June 1975.

Chenery, Hollis B. & Keesing, Donald B.: THE CHANGING

COMPOSITION OF DEVELOPING COUNTRY EXPORTS. (Mimeo 1978)

Clark, J.B.: THE DISTRIBUTION OF WEALTH. London 1899.

van Cleveland, Harold B. & Huertas, Thomas F.: 'Stagflation' in FOREIGN AFFAIRS, Vol. 58 No. 1, 1979.

de Closets, François: LA FRANCE ET SES MENSONGES. Editions Denoel, Paris 1977.

Cloward, Richard A. & Ohlin, Lloyd E.: DELINQUENCY AND OPPORTUNITY. Glencoe 1960.

Colson, Elisabeth: TRADITION AND CONTRACT: THE PROBLEM OF ORDER. Heinemann, London 1975.

Cooper, Richard: THE ECONOMICS OF INTERDEPENDENCE. McGraw-Hill, New York 1968.

Commissariat Général du Plan: RAPPORT DU GROUPE CHARGE D'ETUDIER L'EVOLUTION DES ECONOMIES DU TIERS-MONDE ET L'APPAREIL PRODUCTIF FRANÇAIS. Paris 1978.

Crozier, Michel: THE STALLED SOCIETY. Viking Press, New York 1973.

Crozier, Michel; Huntington, Samuel P. & Watanuki, J.: THE CRISIS OF DEMOCRACY. New York University Press, New York 1975.

Cukor, György: STRATEGIES FOR INDUSTRIALIZATION IN DEVELOPING COUNTRIES. St. Martin's Press, New York 1974.

Diaz-Alejandro, Carlos F.: 'International Markets for LDCs — The Old and the New', AMERICAN ECONOMIC REVIEW, Vol. 68 No. 2, May 1978.

Elander, Ingemar: 'DEN SVENSKA MODELLEN' — RECEPT AVEN FOR 80-TALET. Paper published by the Swedish Secretariat for Future Studies, Stockholm.

Engellau, Patrik & Nygren, Birgitta: LAN UTAN GRANSER. Swedish Secretariat for Future Studies, Stockholm 1979.

Ensor, Richard: THE AMERICAN ECONOMY: A REAPPRAISAL. The Hudson Letter. A special report. London 1977.

THE EUROPEAN ECONOMIC COMMUNITY AND CHANGES IN THE INTERNATIONAL DIVISION OF LABOUR. Commission of the European Communities. Directorate-General for Development, Brussels, January 1979.

Fong, Pan Eng & Lim, Linda: THE ELECTRONICS INDUSTRY IN SINGAPORE: STRUCTURE, TECHNOLOGY, AND LINKAGES. ERC Monograph Series No. 7. Economic Research Centre, University of Singapore.

Freeman, Christopher: THE ECONOMICS OF INDUSTRIAL INNOVATION. Penguin Books, Harmondsworth 1974.

Freud, David: 'A Guide to Underground Economics', FINANCIAL TIMES, 9 April 1979.

GATT: INTERNATIONAL TRADE 1977/78. Geneva 1978.

Gerschenkron, A.: ECONOMIC BACKWARDNESS IN HISTORICAL PERSPECTIVE. Harvard University Press, Cambridge, Mass. 1962.

Gershuny, Jonathan: AFTER INDUSTRIAL SOCIETY: THE EMERGING SELF-SERVICE ECONOMY. Macmillan, London 1978.

Giersch, Herbert: PROBLEMS OF ADJUSTMENTS TO IMPORTS FROM LESS DEVELOPED COUNTRIES. Paper presented to the symposium 'The Past and Prospects of the Economic World Order', Saltsjobaden, Sweden, August 25-28, 1978.

Giersch, Herbert: RESHAPING THE WORLD ECONOMIC ORDER. Symposium 1976. Institut fur Weltwirtschaft an der Universität Kiel. J.C.B. Mohr (Paul Siebeck), Tubingen.

Glyn, Andrew & Sutcliffe, Bob: BRITISH CAPITALISM, WORKERS, AND THE PROFITS SQUEEZE. Penguin Books, Harmondsworth 1975.

Gordon, Robert J. & Pelkmans, Jacques: CHALLENGES TO INTERDEPENDENT ECONOMIES: THE INDUSTRIAL WEST IN THE COMING DECADE. 1980s Project/Council on Foreign Relations. McGraw-Hill, New York 1979.

Grubel, Herbert G. & Lloyd, P.J.: INTRA INDUSTRY TRADE: THE THEORY AND MEASUREMENT OF INTERNATIONAL TRADE IN DIFFERENTIATED PRODUCTS. Macmillan, London 1975.

Gullbrandsen, Odd: THE EVOLUTION OF INTERNATIONAL

DIVISION OF LABOUR in Vägar till ökad välfärd. Särskilda näringspolitiska delegationen. (Report from a panel of experts appointed by the Swedish government) (Ds Ju 1979:2 Expertbilaga).

Hamilton, Carl: De nya industrilanderna — hot eller lofte?, EKONOMISK DEBATT 1979:3.

Hamilton, Carl: Tillvaxt och inkomstfordelning i de nya industrilanderna, EKONOMISK DEBATT 1979:5.

Harmon, Willis: A TENTATIVE INTERPRETATION OF THE PRESENT DECADE. Appendix to hearings before the Subcommittee on Energy and Power. Ninety-fourth Congress, March 25 and 26, 1976. Serial No. 94-65.

Harris, Marvin: CANNIBALS & KINGS: THE ORIGIN OF CULTURES. Fontana/Collins, Glasgow 1977.

Healey, Denis: Oil, Money, and Recession, FOREIGN AFFAIRS, Vol. 58, 1979/80 No. 2.

Helleiner, G.K.: INTRAFIRM TRADE AND THE DEVELOPING COUNTRIES. An assessment of data (Mimeo 1978).

Helleiner, G.K.: STRUCTURAL ASPECTS OF THE THIRD WORLD TRADE: SOME TRENDS AND SOME PROSPECTS (Mimeo 1978).

Hellspong, Mats & Löfgren, Orvar: LAND OCH STAD. SVENSKA SAMHALLSTYPER OCH LIVSFORMER FRAN MEDELTID TILL NUTID. CWK Gleerup Bokförlag, Lund 1972.

Herin, Jan: DEN INTERNATIONELLA KONJUNKTURUTVECKLINGEN OCH STRUKTUROMVANDLINGEN in Vägar till ökad välfärd. Särskilda näringspolitiska delegationen (Ds Ju 1979:1). (Report from a panel of experts appointed by the Swedish government).

Hirsch, Fred: SOCIAL LIMITS TO GROWTH. Routledge & Kegan Paul, London 1977.

Hirsch, Fred & Goldthorpe, John: THE POLITICAL ECONOMY OF INFLATION. Martin Robertson, London 1978.

Hobsbawm, E.J.: THE AGE OF CAPITAL. Charles Scribner's Sons, New York 1975.

Hoffmann, Stanley: The Uses of American Power, FOREIGN AFFAIRS, Vol. 56 No. 1, October 1977.

Hollander, Ernst & Tegen, Andreas: MINERALMAKT — DE TRANSNATIONELLA FORETAGENS KONTROLL OVER VARLDENS ICKE FORNYELSEBARA RAVAROR. Paper published by the Swedish Secretariat for Future Studies, Stockholm.

Hudson, Michael, GLOBAL FRACTURE. Harper & Row, New York 1977.

IBRD: WORLD TABLES. Washington 1976.

IBRD: ANNUAL REPORT 1978. Washington 1978.

IMF: SURVEY. Washington, 9 January 1978.

IMF: INTERNATIONAL FINANCIAL STATISTICS. May 1978.

IMF: INTERNATIONAL FINANCIAL STATISTICS. February 1979.

INFLATION AND UNEMPLOYMENT: A NEW ERA. The Hudson Letter. A special report prepared by Richard Ensor and Catherine Langlois. Hudson Research Europe Ltd., Paris 1976.

Inglehart, Ronald: THE SILENT REVOLUTION: CHANGING VALUES AND POLITICAL STYLES AMONG WESTERN PUBLICS. Princeton University Press, Princeton 1977.

INTERFUTURES: FACING THE FUTURE. MASTERING THE PROBABLE AND MANAGING THE UNPREDICTABLE. OECD, Paris 1979.

Janowitz, Morris: THE LAST HALF-CENTURY: SOCIETAL CHANGE AND POLITICS IN AMERICA. University of Chicago Press, Chicago and London 1978.

Keegan, Victor: 'Any answer to the no-questions-asked economy', GUARDIAN, 8 April, 1979.

Keesing, Donald B.: WORLD TRADE AND OUTPUT OF MANUFACTURES: STRUCTURAL TRENDS AND DEVELOPING COUNTRIES' EXPORTS. (Staff Working paper from the World Bank, 2 February 1978).

Kemp, Tom: TEORIER OM IMPERIALISMEN. Rabén & Sjögren, Stockholm 1972.

Keynes, J.M.: 'National Self-Sufficiency', YALE REVIEW, Vol. 22, Summer 1933.

Kierzkowski, Henry K.: DISPLACEMENT OF LABOUR BY IMPORTS OF MANUFACTURES. Institute for International Economic Studies in Stockholm (Mimeo).

Kissinger, Henry: NATO — THE NEXT THIRTY YEARS. Europe: Agence Internationale d'Information pour la Presse, Brussels, 11 September 1979.

Kohr, Leopold: THE BREAKDOWN OF NATIONS. E.P. Dutton, New York 1978.

Kolko, Gabriel: THE POLITICS OF WAR: THE WORLD AND THE UNITED STATES FOREIGN POLICY 1943-45. Vintage Books, New York 1970.

Kostecki, M.M.: 'State Trading in Industrialized and Developing Countries', JOURNAL OF WORLD TRADE LAW.

Kreinin, Mordechai: INTERNATIONAL ECONOMICS: A POLICY APPROACH. Second edition, Harcourt Brace Jovanovich, New York 1975.

Kristensen, Thorkil: THE NATURE OF THE PRESENT INTERNATIONAL CRISIS. IFIAS. Ulriksdal. Lecture No. 2. Allhems Förlag, Malmö 1978.

Kumar, Krishan: PROPHECY AND PROGRESS: THE SOCIOLOGY OF INDUSTRIAL AND POST-INDUSTRIAL SOCIETY. Penguin Books, Harmondsworth 1978.

Ladd, Everett Carll, Jr.: 'The Riddle of the 'Tax Revolt', ECONOMIC IMPACT, No. 27, 1979.

Laestadius, Staffan: DEN INTERNATIONELLA ARBETSFORDELNINGEN OCH FRIZONERNA. Swedish Secretariat for Future Studies, Stockholm 1979.

Laestadius, Staffan: PRODUKTION UTAN GRANSER. Swedish Secretariat for Future Studies, Stockholm 1980.

Lall, Sanjaya & Streeten, Paul: FOREIGN INVESTMENTS, TRANSNATIONALS AND DEVELOPING COUNTRIES. Macmillan Press, London 1977.

Landes, D.S.: THE UNBOUND PROMETHEUS: TECHNOLOGICAL CHANGE AND INDUSTRIAL DEVELOPMENT IN WESTERN EUROPE FROM 1750 TO THE PRESENT. Cambridge University Press, Cambridge 1969.

Landsorganisationen i Sverige: SAMORDNAD NARINGSPOLITIK. Stockholm 1961. Report from Sweden's Trade

Union Council.

Laqueur, Walter: A CONTINENT ASTRAY: EUROPE 1970-78. Oxford University Press, New York and Oxford 1979.

Lasch, Christopher: HAVEN IN A HEARTLESS WORLD: THE FAMILY BESIEGED. Basic Books, 1979.

Lewis, Arthur: THE RATE OF GROWTH OF WORLD TRADE 1830-1973. Institute for International Economic Studies, Stockholm 1978.

Lewis, Ioan M.: SOCIAL ANTHROPOLOGY IN PERSPECTIVE. Penguin Books, Harmondsworth 1977.

Lipset, S.M.: POLITICAL MAN. Mercury Books, London 1963.

Maizels, Alfred: INDUSTRIAL GROWTH AND WORLD TRADE. Cambridge University Press, Cambridge 1963.

Matthews, Christopher: 'Underground' Workers Keep Italian Economy Running', NATIONAL HERALD TRIBUNE, 5 February 1979.

FROM MARSHALL PLAN TO GLOBAL INTERDEPENDENCE: NEW CHALLENGES FOR THE INDUSTRIALIZED COUNTRIES. OECD, Paris 1978.

THE MEDITERRANEAN GROWTH AND INVESTMENT AREA. The Hudson Letter. A special report. Hudson Research Europe Ltd., Paris 1975.

Minian, Isaac: 'TECHNICAL PROGRESS AND THE INTERNATIONALIZATION OF THE PRODUCTION PROCESS. The Case of the "Maquiladora" Industry of the Electronic Type'. Mimeo from Centre for Research and Teaching of Economics, Mexico City, April 1978.

Morton, Kathryn & Tulloch, Peter: TRADE AND DEVELOPING COUNTRIES. Croom Helm, London 1977.

THE NEWLY INDUSTRIALIZING COUNTRIES AND THE ADJUSTMENT PROBLEM. Government Economic Service Working Paper No. 18. Foreign and Commonwealth Office, London, January 1979.

Noelke, Michael: DOSSIER SUR L'INTERDEPENDENCE EUROPE — TIERS MONDE. Commission des Communautés Europeennes: Document de Travail, 481/X/78, Brussels, 28 August 1978.

Noelke, Michael: EUROPE — TIERS MONDE. LE DOSSIER DE L'INTERDEPENDENCE. Collection Dossiers. Série developpement no 2. Brussels, February 1979.

OECD: ECONOMIC OUTLOOK. Paris, November 1978.
OECD: FINANCIAL STATISTICS. No 11, part 1. Paris 1979.
OECD: FINANCIAL STATISTICS. No 12, part 1. Paris 1979.

Paretti, V. & Bloch G.: 'Industrial Production in Western Europe and the United States 1901-1955', BANCA NAZIONALE DEL LAVORO QUARTERLY REVIEW No 39, 1956.
Parkin, Frank: CLASS INEQUALITY & POLITICAL ORDER. MacGibbon & Kee, London 1971.
Payer, Cheryl, ed.: COMMODITY TRADE OF THE THIRD WORLD. Macmillan, London 1975.
Pollard, Sidney: THE IDEA OF PROGRESS: HISTORY AND SOCIETY. Penguin Books, Harmondsworth 1971.
Pratten, C.F.: LABOUR PRODUCTIVITY DIFFERENTIALS WITHIN INTERNATIONAL COMPANIES. University of Cambridge. Cambridge University Press, Cambridge 1976.

Rawls, John: A THEORY OF JUSTICE. Harvard University Press, Cambridge, Mass. 1971.
Robinson, Austin: FIFTY YEARS OF COMMONWEALTH ECONOMIC DEVELOPMENT. Smuts Memorial Lecture. Cambridge University Press, Cambridge 1972.
Rolfe, Sidney E.: DET INTERNATIONELLA FORETAGET. Wahlström & Widstrand, Stockholm 1972.
Rothschild, K.W. ed.: POWER IN ECONOMICS. Penguin Books, Harmondsworth 1971.
Routh, Guy: THE ORIGIN OF ECONOMIC IDEAS. Vintage Books, New York 1977.

Salera, Virgil: MULTINATIONAL BUSINESS. Houghton Mifflin, Boston 1969.
Schiller, Herbert I.: COMMUNICATION AND CULTURAL DOMINATION. M.E. Sharpe, Inc./White Plains, New York 1976.
Shonfield, Andrew: 'The Politics of the Mixed Economy in the

International System of the 1970s', INTERNATIONAL AFFAIRS January 1980, pp.

Scitovsky, Tibor: THE JOYLESS ECONOMY. AN INQUIRY INTO HUMAN SATISFACTION AND CONSUMER DISSATISFACTION. Oxford University Press, New York 1977.

Solomon, Robert: THE INTERNATIONAL MONETARY SYSTEM 1945-76. AN INSIDER'S VIEW. Harper & Row, New York 1977.

STRUCTURE AND CHANGE IN EUROPEAN INDUSTRY. Secretariat of the Economic Commission for Europe, United Nations, New York 1977.

TEKNIK OCH INDUSTRISTRUKTUR — 70-TALETS EKONOMISKA KRIS I HISTORISK BELYSNING. Industrins utredningsinstitut/Ingenjorsvetenskapsakademien. Almqvist & Wiksell, Stockholm 1979. (Report from the research institute of the Swedish Federation of industries).

Thurow, Lester C.: THE ZERO-SUM SOCIETY. Basic Books, New York 1980.

THE TIMES HISTORY OF OUR TIMES. Ed. Marcus Cunliffe. Weidenfeld and Nicolson, London 1971.

Tingsten, Herbert: DEN SVENSKA SOCIALDEMOKRATINS IDEUTVECKLING. Del 1. Tidens Förlag, Stockholm 1941.

TOWARDS FULL EMPLOYMENT AND PRICE STABILITY. A report to the OECD by a group of independent experts. OECD, Paris, June 1977.

Tuchman, Barbara: DET STOLTA TORNET. Forum, Stockholm 1966.

Tucker, Robert W.: THE INEQUALITY OF NATIONS. Basic Books, New York 1977.

Tufte, Edward R.: POLITICAL CONTROL OF THE ECONOMY. Princeton University Press, Princeton 1980.

Tugendhat, Christopher: 'Why US Companies Abandon Their European Headquarters', FINANCIAL TIMES, April 1969.

UNCTAD: HANDBOOK OF INTERNATIONAL TRADE AND DEVELOPMENT STATISTICS 1976. United Nations TD/Stat. 6, New York 1976.

UNCTAD: HANDBOOK OF INTERNATIONAL TRADE AND

DEVELOPMENT STATISTICS. SUPPLEMENT 1977. United Nations, TD/Stat. 7, New York 1978.

UNCTAD: TRANSNATIONAL CORPORATIONS AND EXPANSION OF TRADE IN MANUFACTURES AND SEMI-MANUFACTURES. TD/B/C.2/197, Geneva, 16 March 1978.

UNIDO: THE IMPACT OF TRADE WITH DEVELOPING COUNTRIES ON EMPLOYMENT IN DEVELOPED COUNTRIES. EMPIRICAL EVIDENCE FROM RECENT RESEARCH. UNIDO/ICIS.85, 23 October 1978.

UNIDO: WORLD INDUSTRY SINCE 1960. PROGRESS AND PROSPECTS. United Nations, New York 1979.

United Nations: MULTINATIONAL CORPORATIONS IN WORLD DEVELOPMENT. New York 1973.

United Nations: TRANSNATIONAL CORPORATIONS IN WORLD DEVELOPMENT: A RE-EXAMINATION. E/C.10/38, 20 March 1978.

United Nations: WORLD ECONOMIC SURVEY 1961. New York 1961.

United Nations: WORLD ECONOMIC SURVEY, SUPPLEMENT TO, 1978. New York 1978.

Vickers, Geoffrey: FREEDOM IN A ROCKING BOAT. CHANGING VALUES IN AN UNSTABLE SOCIETY. Penguin Books, Harmondsworth 1972.

Weber, Max: GENERAL ECONOMIC HISTORY. Collier-Macmillan, New York 1966.

THE WEST GERMAN OUTLOOK TODAY. The Hudson Letter. A special report by Laurence Schloesing. Hudson Research Europe Ltd., Paris 1976.

Whitman, Marina V.N.: SUSTAINING THE INTERNATIONAL ECONOMIC SYSTEM: ISSUES FOR US POLICY. Essays on International Finance, No. 121. Princeton, N.J. June 1977.

Wilkins, Myra: THE MATURING OF MULTINATIONAL ENTERPRISES: AMERICAN BUSINESS FROM 1914 TO 1970. Harvard University Press, Cambridge, Mass. 1975.

WORLD BANK ATLAS 1975. World Bank, Washington D.C. 1975.

WORLD DEVELOPMENT REPORT 1978. World Bank, Washington D.C. August 1978.

WORLD DEVELOPMENT REPORT 1979. World Bank, Washington D.C. 1979.

WORLD ECONOMIC OUTLOOK. A Survey by the Staff of the International Monetary Fund. Washington D.C. May 1980.

WORLD TRADE AND THE INTERNATIONAL ECONOMY: TRENDS, PROSPECTS, AND POLICIES. World Bank Staff Working Paper No. 282. Washington D.C. May 1978.

WORLD TRADE AND OUTPUT OF MANUFACTURES: STRUCTURAL TRENDS AND DEVELOPING COUNTRIES' EXPORTS. World Bank Staff Working Paper No. 316. Washington D.C. January 1979.

Yamazaki, Ryuso: PROSPECTS FOR THE AUTOMOTIVE INDUSTRY. La Hülpe Seminar, IBM 1979.

Young, Michael & Wilmott, Peter: THE SYMMETRICAL FAMILY. Penguin Books, London 1975.

APPENDIX 1

Changes in the geographical pattern of trade

The diagrams on the following pages are an attempt to illustrate as briefly as possible some features of the changes in the geographical pattern of trade during the postwar period. A few important facts are immediately manifest:

- The industrial countries are the predominant exporters of all commodity groups except fuels. For products of manufacturing industry the share of the OECD countries has been above 80 per cent of total world production during the entire postwar period. For primary commodities, excluding fuels, the present proportion is rather more than 50 per cent — and has increased fairly considerably since the beginning of the sixties
- For all commodity groups except fuels the internal trade of the industrial countries represents a very considerable proportion (40-55 per cent) of the total trade
- The industrial countries' net import of other primary commodities than fuels is successively diminishing
- The industrial countries' dependence on the Third World consists almost entirely in their need to import oil
- The developing countries' importance as a market for manufactures from the industrial countries fell very significantly from the beginning of the fifties up to 1970, chiefly because the former's purchasing power was reduced owing to falling commodity prices from 1951 to 1962. During the seventies their importance increased, chiefly because of the very greatly increased imports of the OPEC states
- The internal trade of the developing countries is normally fairly small. For fuels it is about 15 per cent of the total

171

Diagram a: World merchandise exports by areas 1953, 1963, 1970, and 1976 (current prices)

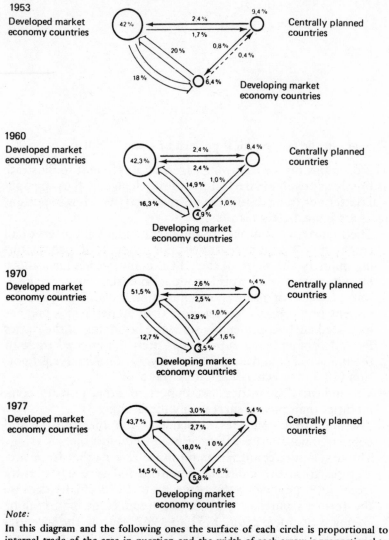

Note:

In this diagram and the following ones the surface of each circle is proportional to internal trade of the area in question and the width of each arrow is proportional to the trade between the areas in question. The figures indicate the share of total world trade.

Sources:

UNCTAD: *Handbook 1964*, tables 30-35 for 1953 and Herin, pp. 27-35 for 1960, 1970, and 1977 for diagrams a-e)

Diagram b: World exports of food* by areas 1953, 1963, 1970, and 1976 (current prices)

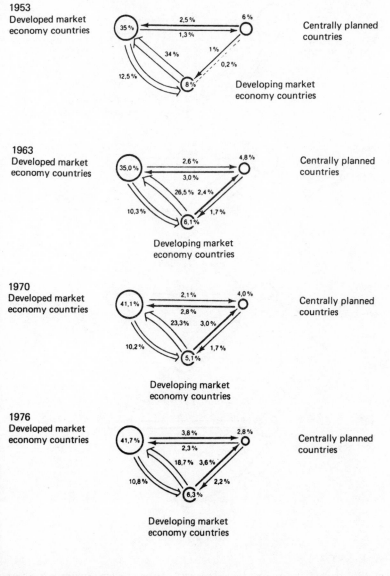

1953
Developed market
economy countries

Centrally planned
countries

Developing market
economy countries

1963
Developed market
economy countries

Centrally planned
countries

Developing market
economy countries

1970
Developed market
economy countries

Centrally planned
countries

Developing market
economy countries

1976
Developed market
economy countries

Centrally planned
countries

Developing market
economy countries

ood includes SITC classes 0, 1, and 4, and section 22. For 1953, however, only
TC 0 and 1 are included.

WE&CWO - M

Diagram c: World exports of fuels* by areas 1953, 1963, 1970, and 1976 (current prices)

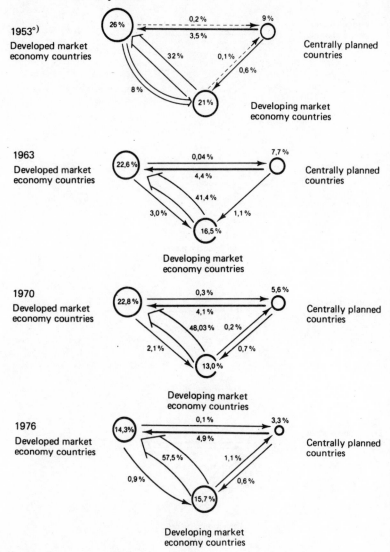

* Includes SITC 3.

°) For 1953 part of the exports from developed market-economy countries has been randomly distributed among different markets.

Diagram d: World exports of other primary commodities* by areas 1953, 1963, 1970, and 1976 (current prices)

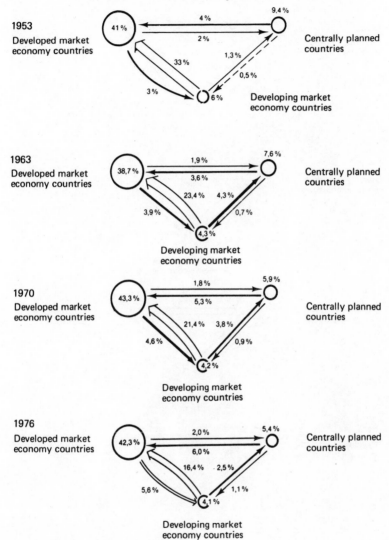

* Includes SITC 2, with the exception of section 22. For 1953, however, section 22 is included together with SITC class 4.

Diagram e: World exports of manufactures* by areas 1953, 1963, 1970, and 1976 (current prices)

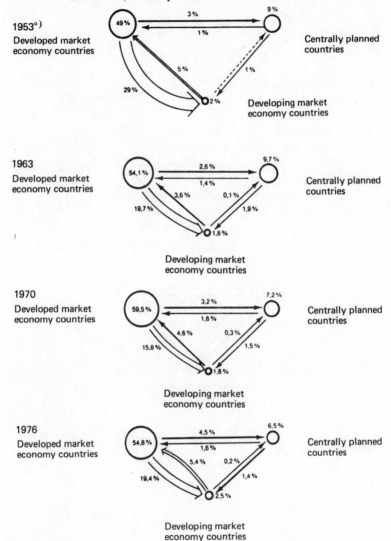

* Includes SITC 5–8.

°) Part of the exports from developed market-economy countries is not recorded for specific destinations in the UN statistics. In this diagram the unrecorded part has been distributed among internal trade and exports to other areas on an estimated basis. Figures for 1953 in particular should be treated with some care.

trade, for other primary commodities 4–6 per cent, and for manufactures only 2.5 per cent
— The developing countries' exports go chiefly to the industrial countries, roughly three-quarters to the OECD area. Sales to the Eastern bloc states are extremely small and have not changed
— The developing countries' food export surplus is steadily diminishing. This is chiefly because several countries have large and growing need for imports of cereals. In respect of cereals themselves, an earlier large export surplus for the developing countries has changed into a considerable deficit
— Centrally planned countries are weakly integrated in the capitalist world economy. The internal trade of the COMECON block in all commodity groups predominates over its trade with the rest of the world. A change is, however, distinguishable in one field. Imports of manufactures from, but also exports to, OECD countries have increased since the early sixties distinctly more quickly than the trade within Eastern Europe
— Despite this increase the trade in industrial products between the OECD countries, with 60 per cent of the world's industry, and countries with planned economy, with about 30 per cent, constitutes only 6 per cent of the total world trade in products of the manufacturing industry.

The picture shown in the diagrams is thus the well-known one. The industrial countries exchange a large surplus of manufactures for the developing countries' primary commodities. The centrally planned countries are very cautious in their relations with the surrounding world.

As appears from Table A the industrial countries have a deficit of trade in all primary commodities — but a large surplus of exports of industrial products. The trade pattern of the developing countries is the opposite of that of the industrial countries — it almost exactly balances their surpluses and deficits in all commodity groups.

The centrally planned countries are apparently striving for a certain balance in their trade both in total and for individual commodity groups. During the seventies, however, they had a considerable deficit in their trade in foodstuffs and manufactured goods, which was offset by income from oil exports.

INDEX